A LIFE IN CONTRAST

Thoughts from the Sermon on the Mount

Matthew 5 - 7

Todd Thomas

CONTENTS

This book is dedicated to my dad,

Billy Ray Thomas

1935-2017

FORWARD

My web browser reports 1.66 million hits searching the phrase: "books on the Sermon on the Mount." Just how many books on this sermon have been written is probably incalculable, but I'm glad Todd Thomas has written one more.

The *Sermon on the Mount* is itself simplicity on the other side of complexity. Jesus' words are at once both simple and profound. As Thomas points out, this isn't just another sermon, this is **the** Sermon of all sermons – Jesus' sermon for the ages. The unique power of the *Sermon on the Mount* is its easily grasped principles, while its profound implications require a life-time of study.

Every generation needs to revisit the *Sermon on the Mount's* truths so that they can be expressed in fresh and easily understood language, with relatable and relevant stories. *A Life in Contrast* does just that because it is born out of Thomas' heart, as he wrestles with ways to relate the timeless truth of the *Sermon on the Mount* to today's hearers through the remarkable depth and insight of his pastoral heart.

Thomas is a deep thinker who effectively ponders the meaning of the Scriptures. His *first hearer* method is refreshing and a key to discern the *Sermon's* original intent. This method of exegesis opens the door to an even more faithful obedience for today's reader. Thomas does us a favor. His wrestling brings out important affirmations of God's character, and clear expressions of God's desire...how a life lived in the Kingdom is in true contrast to the way of the world.

A Life in Contrast is devotional, thoughtful, and inspirational. I highly recommend it to be read at a leisurely and thoughtful pace. *A Life in Contrast* is for the reader who wants to make serious personal application of the words of Jesus' great sermon – application which is needed now more than ever.

Phil Fuller
District Superintendent, Virginia District, Church of the
Nazarene

INTRODUCTION

Throughout my life I have heard the Sermon on the Mount declared as the greatest sermon ever preached. Even so, I have yet to see that Sermon used in a preaching class as an example of hermeneutical process. If a preacher of today stood before other preachers and delivered a message patterned after this Sermon it would not be received as a classical sermon. Such a sermon would have too many topics, too little subject matter for each topic, with an indistinct introduction and no working conclusion. The critique would not be flattering. In a preaching class such a sermon might not receive a passing grade.

Why do we insist that this Sermon, found in **Matthew 5-7**, is the greatest sermon ever preached?

The answer we are most likely to give, the spiritual answer, is that everything Jesus did had to be the best. He is Jesus, after all.

Could the real answer be found in the impact this Sermon had upon the crowd? **"When Jesus had finished saying these things, the crowds were amazed at his teaching, *because he taught as one who had authority*, and not as their teachers of the law." (Matthew 7:28-29; *emphasis added*)**

Jesus speaks with authority; he speaks as one who had the right to show up and take charge, not as one who has information to dispense. His words are to be received as the

1

Manifesto of a King, not as the expressed opinion of a learned peer. There is an inherent power in these words. These words are concise and decisive. These words demand response: a listener cannot hear these words and remain neutral. A choice must be made.

N. T. Wright offers this insight:

> "Jesus' way of running the world here and now is, however surprisingly, through his followers. The heart of their life is Spirit-led worship, through which they are constituted and energized as 'the body of Christ.' The agenda which follows from this is set by those memorable sayings we call the Beatitudes, which offer a vantage point from which to explore the ways in which the project of God's kingdom, which Jesus announced and which he believed would be accomplished through his death, can become a reality not only *in* the lives of his followers, but *through* the lives of his followers." [1]

While I make no claim to be a first century historian, I have attempted to hear and understand the Sermon on the Mount from an historical context. Remembering that Jesus was not talking to me but to the disciples, I ask these questions: What historical events influenced how the first listeners heard and

---

[1] N. T. Wright, *Simply Jesus: A New Vision of Who He Was, What He Did, and Why He Matters*, (NY, NY: HarperCollins Publishers, 2011), All rights reserved. From the preface. Emphasis is the work of the author.

understood this Sermon? How does this historical understanding impact my life?   How are these words of Jesus to be translated into my life location? After understanding what Jesus said *to them,* how can I make these truths apply *to me*?

It is important to enter the world of Jesus' day before claiming any understanding of the truths he taught.

As a consequence of this approach, my treatment of the Beatitudes will be at variance with the sequential approach I have heard all my life: being poor in spirit leads to mourning, which in turn will leads to meekness, etc. The Beatitudes are not a check list of items that can be given a historical and experiential point in time. They express the character of those who are citizens in Christ's Kingdom.

I believe the Sermon on the Mount is the grace-counterpart to the Old Testament covenant through the Law. In the Old Testament, the Law forms the basis for a covenantal relationship with God. The Law provides the means for the establishing of a new way of life and enables a people who had never known freedom to learn to live in community and bless the world. The Sermon on the Mount begins with "blessed are", which establishes the foundation of covenantal relationship (see more details on this thought in the chapter "Beatitudes"); the balance of the Sermon provides details on how to live as a free people in community and to be a blessing to the world.

Jesus does not present himself as a starry-eyed mystic, speaking of an ill-defined utopia to come somewhere, sometime. Jesus has already presented himself to that region as one who is in charge. His preaching declares the Kingdom of heaven (a term the first century Jewish listeners would have understood far differently than most of us) is near (**Matthew 4:17**). He announces himself as the expected Messiah (**Luke 4:16-21**). An attempt on his life has already been tried (**Luke 4:28-30**). He has only recently selected 12 followers, an action which signals the beginnings of a kingdom campaign (**Luke 6:12-16**).

This Sermon is more than a message of a futuristic or millennial kingdom. This Sermon is a right-now, right-here Kingdom declaration, a statement: "this is how life looks when God is in charge." This Sermon appeals to the common man and is an affront to the religious and political hierarchy.

Consider this quote from Eric M. Vail, associate professor of theology at Mount Vernon Nazarene University:

> "The arrival of the kingdom of God through Jesus Christ is the gospel. Jesus delivered this message about the kingdom's presence again and again. Jesus spoke about gaining the kingdom as a reward for being faithful and its loss as the consequence of infidelity. Christ taught the disciples to seek after the kingdom, to pray for the coming of the kingdom, to proclaim the nearness of the kingdom and about the nature of the kingdom. The kingdom, according to

Jesus, is not a far-off reality. It is near. It is present. For first century Jews in particular, this announcement meant the continuing, earthy effects of their exile had finally come to an end." [2]

I preached through this Sermon from mid-summer of 2015 into the Fall of 2016. I experienced the power of Christ's authority as His words called me to a life in contrast with the systems of the world around me; a life of repentance, surrender, and a radical reevaluation of what it means to be a follower of Christ.

My prayerful hope is that I can communicate the power of this Sermon through the pages of this book.

Following each chapter will be a few *Questions for Reflection*. These questions are meant to enable the reader to apply the lessons of each chapter into the context and culture of their spiritual, personal, relational, and professional life.

I am indebted to Christ who called me.

I have been encouraged by my wife to put my thoughts to paper: she believes by doing so other's lives will be impacted as mine has been.

---

[2] Eric M. Vail, *Atonement and Salvation; the Extravagance of God's Love,* (Kansas City, MO: Beacon Hill Press, 2016), pgs. 31-32.

I owe an expression of deep gratitude to the good people of Timberville Church of the Nazarene, Timberville, Virginia, who listened with interest to the messages of this series week after week.

Thank you to Dr. Phil Fuller, District Superintendent of the Church of the Nazarene for the District of Virginia, for his thoughtful input and support.

Thank you to Dr. Bob Broadbooks, Regional Director for USA and Canada, Church of the Nazarene, for his input and words of encouragement.

Thank you to Kerry Willis, District Superintendent, Philadelphia District, Church of the Nazarene for his kind words and support.

Many of my friends and colleagues offered words of encouragement for which I am grateful.

IT BEGINS

Matthew 5

"Now when he saw the crowds, he went up on a mountainside and sat down. His disciples came to him, and he began to teach them, saying:" (vss. 1-2)

Up the western shores of the Sea of Galilee at about one thousand feet elevation is a large grassy area. This is a level area with two large outcroppings before and behind known as the "Horns of Hattin." The geology of this area provides a natural amphitheater and will accommodate a large crowd. Jesus, in an act of subtle wisdom, chooses this place of natural beauty and acoustics to present the principles of Kingdom living.

I can see Jesus taking a seat and inviting the disciples to do the same. The curious crowd would have gathered around with expectation. Even local fishermen, seeing the activity, might have rowed to shore and abandoned their boats in hopes of being part of something interesting.

As a tense quietness settles on the crowd, some whispered words of recognition. Hadn't they bought fish from those two guys to the Teacher's right? That other guy, the one in the front, hadn't he taken all they had to pay their taxes a few months ago? The crowd realizes they had shopped in the same markets, traded goods and services, even participated in worship with the men gathered around Jesus. Nods of recognition continue rippling through the crowd accompanied by an unspoken yet understood question: what could cause these neighbors, friends, relatives, to leave everything and follow this Jesus? What is the appeal? What is the cost? Is there any explanation to justify such an extreme life decision?

Silence begins to settle as the crowd leans forward and strains to hear what this Teacher will say to those whom he has called to follow Him.

We are being invited to lean forward and listen. And we, like the crowd that day, are going to be startled by what we hear.

THE BEATITUDES

"Blessed are…"

Some translations replace the concept of being blessed with the much weaker concept of being happy. The *Common English Bible, Good News Bible,* and the *Good News Translation* are examples of such translations. The idea of being happy resonates with us and makes it easy to interpret the Beatitudes as secrets to a happy life; in so doing we miss the dramatic power of these statements.

Among the ancient Jews, pronouncing a blessing was a powerful and deeply significant event. Pronouncing a blessing was an event reserved for a patriarch, priest or king. A patriarch pronounced blessing over his descendants; a priest pronounced blessing over an individual; and a king pronounced blessing over the people.

Pronouncing a blessing was never a ritual meant to convey best wishes. Such a pronouncement was never meant to express a hope that someone would simply be happy.

Pronouncement of blessing was a powerful and life-changing event.

The pronouncement of blessing was a prophetic moment. By this declaration the patriarch bound the individual to a particular future path. The time of blessing was used to bind the next generation to covenant relationship with the One True God. The patriarch had a deep insight into his descendants and into the covenant of God; by pronouncing the blessing he effectively bound the two together.

The sense of its power is found in the story of **Genesis 27.** Aging Isaac was prepared to give his blessing to his sons Esau and Jacob. By deception, Jacob stole the blessing of the first-born. Esau plunged into a panic: was there not also a blessing for him? Isaac could not recall the blessing nor undo the prophetic power of the blessing given to Jacob. Again, in **Genesis 48-49** is seen the power of blessing. Aging Jacob pronounced blessing over his two grandsons, Ephraim and Manasseh, and over his own sons. This pronouncement of blessing was a prophetic moment. Jacob bound his descendants to the purposes of God by the power of blessing.

When Jesus begins this Sermon with these words **"Blessed are…"**, he is speaking into this ancient practice. He is not simply stating "The path to happiness is…" He is declaring "The way of being bound to the covenant God is…"

Powerful. Significant. Life changing.

1. POVERTY

"Blessed are the poor in spirit..." (vs. 3)

A few in the crowd squint at these words: not because of the light of the sun bearing down on them but because of the light of Truth challenging them, beginning to expose both resistance and longing.

This Teacher begins with an issue of poverty? Of all the things we could expect him to say, *this* was not on the list. could poverty really be the reason those 12 men left everything to follow this Jesus?

By selecting an issue of poverty as the very first item of the Beatitudes, Jesus strikes a nerve among the common people. They lived in simple homes constructed of stone or bricks made of mud. At this time in Palestine, a great number of common people were engaged in some type of agriculture. Other industries include the production of clothing and pottery, construction trades, and fishing. The people suffer from excessive taxation. Historians would refer to this society as a peasant society: a society in which a very small percentage of wealthy individuals make up the ruling class. The path toward wealth is difficult to find and even more difficult to climb.

Among the Romans of that time, there is no strong middle class. Political and military leaders, landowners, and businessmen made up a class of great wealth. The class distinctions dropped to the lower class of the poor and the slaves.

Among the Jews, the chief priests and leading officials of the Temple constitute the upper class. Few common Jews will rise out of humble circumstances to join the upper class.

These first words of Jesus announce that this is no ordinary series of lessons. The religious leaders of that time *never* advocate any type of poverty, spiritual or otherwise. The political powers never embrace legislation of poverty. This first Beatitude comes across as contrary to the culture: poverty of any kind is not seen as a virtue. Poverty is contrary to religious teaching where prosperity is presented as a blessing from God, a teaching with roots in the only point of reference for this first audience – the Old Testament.

Poverty is contrary to much we believe and value, both in our culture and in our religious expression. Poverty is seldom seen as a virtue. We are urged to go forward, to go up, and to reach for the top. We must become bigg*er*, strong*er*, fast*er*, smart*er*, bett*er*, rich*er*: we must have an -*er* in our life. The equation is simple: more + more = better.

We identify *more* as a blessing. When we are promoted at work, when we are given a raise, when we are enabled to buy a house that is *more*, buy a car that is *more*, go on a vacation that is *more*, fill our pantries with *more*, fill our closets with *more*, fill our accounts with *more*, preach to *more* people, sell *more* books or CDs, have *more* people reading our blog, serve on one *more* board, we will stand and testify of the blessings of God and the great opportunities of ministry. From this strange view of *more* we justify our desire for more: we want God's blessings after all. We take the message of *more* and turn it into a religion, a prosperity gospel in which we state that God wants us to be blessed with *more*.

When our perception of *more* is challenged, we immediately cite examples in Scripture of those who had *more*. Abraham, the friend of God. David, a man after God's own heart. Solomon, the one chosen to build the Temple of God. Job, the one favored of God. We argue that there is nothing wrong with having *more* so long as it does not have us.

Right.

Forbes (Bryan Pearson, contributor, 12/22/2016) projected Christmas spending for 2016 would surpass *$1 TRILLION! More...*

According to www.money.cnn.com Americans spent $70.15 *billion* buying lottery tickets in 2015. *More...*

Www.nerdwallet.com reports the average US household carries $132,529 of debt: approximately $16,000 of that is credit card debt. *More...*

Remember the parable of the sower in **Matthew 13**? In that parable Jesus stated **"The one who received the seed that**

fell among the thorns is the man who hears the word, but the worries of this life and the deceitfulness of wealth choke it, making it unfruitful." (vs. 22) The accumulation of stuff has the power to distract our hearts away from the Gospel. Stuff gives us increased worry and a sense of false security, both of which work against living by faith. We must give our attention and energy to protecting, maintaining, and increasing our wealth even as our soul is perishing.

Wealth promises to enable us to have a life. I remember hearing its whispers. There was a point in 1983 when I was making $1,500.00 a week – not bad money for those days (or today for that matter). Rather than leaving my cost of living at its previous level and increasing my generosity into the Kingdom, I listened to the seductive whispers and put my family on the edge of ruin. I had not turned my back upon the Lord or denied my Christian faith but my life had certainly become unfruitful. I am thankful for God's grace and mercy.

I think of the story of the rich young man recorded in **Matthew 19**. When asked to separate himself from his riches he could not. Jesus responded by saying **"I tell you the truth, it is hard for a rich man to enter the kingdom of heaven."** (vs. 23). It is difficult to hold possessions out of heart's reach. It is almost impossible to have wealth and not be possessed by that wealth. Wealth has tentacles that quietly entwine themselves around our allegiance and refuse to release us to another. Accumulation has a way of denying entrance into the very kingdom that our Savior is promising:

"Blessed are the poor in spirit for theirs is the kingdom of heaven."

Consider the words of the Apostle Paul:

> "People who want to get rich fall into temptation and a trap and into many foolish and harmful desires that plunge men into ruin and destruction. For the love of money is the root of all kinds of evil. Some people, eager for money, have wandered from the faith and pierced themselves with many griefs." (1 Timothy 6:9-10)

"Want" "love" "eager" – these are apt descriptions of the power money and accumulation express in our lives.

The attitude of the Scriptures toward the allure of wealth is consistent: it is nearly impossible to keep wealth and our hearts separated. Wealth captures our hearts, our allegiance, our energies, our commitments. Once made a captive, we delude ourselves into believing we are the captors, that our hearts are free, whole, and holy. As wealth and accumulation increase, our arrogance, delusion and selfishness often increase. The love of wealth becomes a consuming cycle of deception. The love of wealth distorts our worldview.

I am deeply convicted by this reality. Even as I type this chapter I am reminded that I have quite a collection of material stuff. Is *my* heart really free? Can I be poor in spirit with all this? Is all this stuff redefining what it means to be "**poor in spirit**"? Has this accumulation of stuff become my identity? How is all this influencing my sanctification?

Ed Young has some good words for us:

> "If we want to experience real success and lasing joy, we need to convert our get-to-get mentality into a get-to-give lifestyle. The only reason God lets us have stuff is so that we can bless others with it. The more we try to hold on to it, the greater the hold *it* has on *us*. Material possessions can only bring you joy if you are able to let them go." [3]

When Jesus declares, **"Blessed are the poor in spirit...,"** He is not addressing the accumulation of wealth or the acquiring of stuff. He is talking about less of *me*. When the attitude of the Scripture is placed into this truth equation we must face a troubling challenge: it is difficult for there to be less of *me* unless there is also a release of stuff, a generosity of spirit that expresses itself by a willingness to give the stuff away. Can there be less of me as my net worth progressively increases? I give lip service to the idea of *less of me,* and yet the energies of my life are spent day after day getting, keeping, and adding to my stuff.

---

[3] Ed Young, *Outrageous, Contagious Joy: Five Big Questions to Help You Discover One Great Life.* (NY, NY: The Berkley Publishing Group, 2007), pg. 25. Emphasis the work of the author.

Americans are plagued by stuff. According to www.sparefoot.com in 2015 there were over 54,000 self-storage units in the US, giving us a total of 2.63 billion square feet of storage at the cost of $32 billion. Approximately 155,000 of these units go to auction each year (www.statisticbrain.com). Stuff gathered. Stuff stored. Stuff lost. We use stuff as the metric by which we measure our success, our personal value, and our status among our peers. It is foolish to deny the impact possession has upon who and what we perceive ourselves to be.

We resist the diminishing of our stuff and at our core we will find even more resistance to *less of me.* We are impressed with ourselves and disguise that in a number of ways; even speak of it in humble terms. We do this by giving others snapshots of our light (**"...let your light shine before men, that they may see your good deeds and praise your Father in heaven." Matthew 5:16...**but I jump ahead).

I well remember a conversation in which a person told me, "I talk to at least 15 people every week..." As that conversation went on it became apparent that those 15 people and what was being said were not the important parts: the most important part I was supposed to understand was this – *he* was the one doing all this. I began to hear the cacophony of self in his words.

I remember sitting in a tent meeting and hearing a man shout out, "I will give another thousand dollars if the quartet will sing another song."

Somewhere, someone remembers hearing my voice declare my own -*er*, my own less than "**poor in spirit**."

Hidden within the subtle deceptions of the heart is a selfish desire for *more* of me: *more* Facebook friends, *more* readers of my personal blog, *more* people in my audience – live or online, *more* attention from the movers and shakers of my denomination. As I work on this book I am hopeful that *more* people will purchase one! We speak of these things in terms of influence, opportunity, or stewardship of gifts.

It is a rare person indeed who can have *more* and be *less.*

Though we would never say it out loud, we believe that God should be impressed with us, take notice, and respond with rewards.

No?

How about this prayer we pray when in a challenging circumstance: "Lord, You know that I have been faithful to read my Bible/pray/give/attend/teach, so why is this happening to me?"

Hmm.

And we are still missing the point.

Max Lucado helps us: "Only a puny god could be bought with tithes. Only an egotistical god would be impressed with our pain. Only a temperamental god could be satisfied with our sacrifices. Only a heartless god would sell salvation to the highest bidders." [4]

In the kingdom of this world we are recognized and rewarded for conquest. Applause comes to winners. We are honored for our sacrifices, hard work, endurance, creative genius, leadership (or manipulative ability): the list is long. It is a sad truth that far too often the church imitates this part of the kingdom of the world and for the same reason – to indicate who is or has more. Lord forgive us.

The voice of Jesus penetrates this chaos and declares: **"Blessed are the poor in spirit…"**

Our carefully constructed world of *more* disintegrates at his words. We must choose: embrace the folly of self-determination by continuing to live in the delusions of our personal resume, or follow the Savior in unreserved surrender and complete dependence.

The Apostle Paul came to understand this in a powerful way. In **Philippians 3** he makes quite an issue of his personal and professional resume. No doubt he found his way to the cover of the *Jerusalem Times* magazine as Man of the Year. Fathers and mothers urged their sons to strive to be like Saul (as Paul was known before his encounter with Christ).

---

[4] Max Lucado. *Applause of Heaven.* (Word Publishing, 1990), pg. 32. Used by permission. All rights reserved.

Legendary stories where told describing the power, prestige and presence of this man. The walls of his office were covered with gilded plaques and awards, all giving indisputable evidence of who and what he claimed to be.

How did his encounter with Christ change his perspective? His own words declare the story:

> **"The very credentials these people are waving around as something special, I'm tearing up and throwing out with the trash – along with everything else I used to take credit for. And why? Because of Christ. Yes, all the things I once thought were so important are gone from my life. Compared to the high privilege of knowing Christ Jesus as my Master, firsthand, everything I once that I had going for me is insignificant – dog dung. I've dumped it all in the trash so that I could embrace Christ and be embraced by him. I didn't want some petty, inferior brand of righteousness that comes from keeping a list of rules when I could get the robust kind that comes from trusting Christ – *God's* righteousness. I gave up all that inferior stuff so I could know Christ personally, experience his resurrection power, be a partner in his suffering, and go all the way with him to death itself. If there was any way to get in on the resurrection from the dead, I wanted to do it."**
> **(Philippians 3:7-11;** TM)

In another place Paul expressed this truth with some finality:

"I have been crucified with Christ and I no longer live, but Christ lives in me. The life I live in the body, I live by faith in the Son of God, who loved me and gave himself for me. I do not set aside the grace of God, for if righteousness could be gained through the law, Christ died for nothing!" (Galatians 2:20-21)

What we have to offer, what we bring to the table, are never make the necessary difference.

It is what Jesus has to give to those who will empty themselves, who will recognize their personal resume has no negotiating worth, who acknowledge their abject failure and inability, who do not march in under their own banner, but enter with *nothing*, under the Cross.

"Theirs is the Kingdom of Heaven."

The Kingdom of Heaven is not some futuristic, mystical something out there somewhere. This is a right-now, from-now, Kingdom; a Kingdom that is already but not yet. This is a Kingdom of love, forgiveness, fellowship, assurance, peace – a Kingdom with no equal and no end.

The Kingdom of Heaven is ruled by the One to whom all authority is given in heaven and on earth. Ruled by the One who died to make the Kingdom accessible to people who are willing to declare themselves bankrupt, to those who are willing to move from applause to obscurity, to those who have stopped bragging and begun begging.

Questions for reflection:

1. What is the dominant view of wealth in our culture?

2. How has that view influenced your own thinking?

3. How has that view influenced Christianity in America?

4. How has that view of wealth redefined the value of a person?

5. In what ways do your views of wealth hinder the development of an unselfish spirit?

6. What actions do you feel are necessary to bring your own life into the blessedness of the "poor in spirit"?

2. BROKENNESS

After being startled by the first words of Christ describing the path of blessedness being a path of less, the disciples, the gathered crowd, and we hear these strange and disturbing words:

"Blessed are those who mourn..." (vs. 4)

With a few words, in less than ten seconds, Jesus exposes a great gulf between worldly living and Kingdom Living. Truth is clarifying that the kingdom of this world and the Kingdom of Christ are incompatible.

First, the issue of poverty: not less stuff, but less and less of *me*.

And now this Teacher declares mourning as a *virtue?!*

There is very little room for misunderstanding the meaning of these words of Jesus. He chooses one of the strongest words for mourning, not a word that could be twisted to mean sadness, melancholy, or a moment of discouragement or depression. To understand the strength of this word we must take a trip back in time.

In the ancient world mourning was a very dramatic and intense event. Garments would be rent, dust would be thrown in the air and there would be fasting of both food and water. All of this would be accompanied by wailing, weeping, beating the chest and a refusal to be comforted. If family or friends could not mourn in a way deemed worthy of the deceased then professional mourners could be hired. It was powerful, deep, and painful.

Jacob mourned for his son Joseph: **"Then Jacob tore his clothes, put on sackcloth and mourned for his son many days." (Genesis 37:34).** When King Ahab heard the words of the prophet Elijah, **"he tore his clothes, put on sackcloth and fasted. He lay in sackcloth and went around meekly." (1 Kings 21:27).** When an edict went out from King Xerxes that all Jews were to be killed the Jews responded with mourning: **"In every province to which the edict and order of the king came, there was great mourning among the Jews, with fasting, weeping and wailing. Many lay in sackcloth and ashes." (Esther 4:3).** The prophet Isaiah wrote: **"The Lord, the LORD Almighty, called you on that day to weep and to wail, to tear out your hair and put on sackcloth." (Isaiah 22:12).** The prophet Joel: **"Even now," declares the LORD, "return to me with all your heart, with fasting and weeping and mourning." (Joel 2:12).** In the New Testament we find these words: **"Grieve, mourn and wail. Change your laughter to mourning and your joy to gloom. Humble yourselves before the Lord, and he will lift you up." (James 4:9)**

Upon hearing God's message through the prophet Jonah, the king of Nineveh put on sackcloth, sat in the dust and made a call for national humiliation and mourning. The people and livestock put on sackcloth and observed a complete fast. They cried out to God and repented of their evil ways.

Mourning was a dramatic and often public act of humiliation, sorrow, and repentance.

Hear it again: **"Blessed are those who mourn…"**

If I were to send out quality invitations to a special event at the church I pastor – an event that would feature a nationally known Southern Gospel group, a renowned speaker, catered food from a notable restaurant, and a few grand door prizes – our simple facilities would never hold the crowd.

Something like this happened recently. A group of local church leaders organized a "Family Fun Day" to be held on a Saturday in the town park. We mailed out almost six thousand high quality post cards to announce this event. Even though the day started out with hard rain and remained overcast, some six hundred people came. Reserving the entire park for the day turned out to be a wise decision.

Had we sent out simple invitations to come to a time of deep humiliation, sincere repentance, and overwhelming sorrow I am confident we would not have needed to reserve more than one pavilion at the park. People all over town would have thrown the invitation away and questioned the wisdom of leadership that would create and advertise such an event. It is possible some would even take personal insult: the invitation would not be well received.

We have been taught to believe that being blessed is like being happy. We seek out those things and those churches that make us feel happy. We place great value on those things which put a smile of our face. Pleasure always trumps pain: we pursue pleasure and avoid anything that might cause pain. We even quote **"A cheerful heart is good medicine" (Proverbs 17:22)**

Hear it again: **"Blessed are those who mourn..."**

Jesus did not say, "Blessed are those who seek happiness, those who live in a place of contented relaxation, those who turn away from sorrow, those who live in denial of brokenness and pain."

When Jesus declares, **"Blessed are those who mourn...,"** He leaves us with certain assumptions. No one mourns over that which is gained. I have yet to meet a person, or be the person, who mourns because of earning a diploma, receiving a promotion at work, paying off the mortgage, celebrating the birth of a grandchild, or being given a meaningful surprise by a spouse.

We mourn the loss of that which is significant.

I remember the day I received that phone call. I was contracted to do some remodeling work and was with the couple in the local home improvement store choosing appropriate materials for the job. My cell phone rang and the caller ID indicated it was my wife. When I answered I was given this message: my younger sister had died unexpectedly earlier that day. At forty years of age she left behind a husband and two teenaged daughters.

A spirit of mourning settled over our family.

I have stood in a hospital room and watched into the early morning hours as a husband walked into the valley of death with his dying wife. I have stood before grieving families again and again, attempting to share their mourning and yet give them comfort. I have worked side by side with a young worship leader who only months before had said goodbye to his young daughter as cancer took her away. I made every effort to share the pain when my wife wept at the bedside of her dying father. I knelt at the bedside of my dying father and told him goodbye.

Loss is real. Mourning is real. Both are inevitable and unavoidable.

Many challenge the goodness and involvement of God when they face loss and mourning. Their spirit breaks, their heart cries out, their mind rages for some explanation, something to bring comfort.

This teaching of Jesus assures us that for those who live a life surrendered to the Kingdom of Christ, mourning brings us into his presence.

Have we forgotten that our Savior was described as a man **"despised and rejected by men, a man of sorrows, and familiar with suffering."? (Isaiah 53:3)**

Have we forgotten how our Savior wept over Jerusalem?

Have we forgotten that our Savior experienced near-fatal sorrow in Gethsemane?

How have we come to believe that the path of following this Savior leads us through places of undisturbed comfort?

How have we come to believe that this Savior leads us down a flower lined trail with sweet aromas lingering in the air?

Can we really walk through this life, following this Savior, and remain unaffected by our own sins, our own faults? I fear we are able to do this because we undervalue grace, over-estimate our own goodness, and neglect the mirror of the Word.

Can we really walk through this life, following this Savior, and remain blissfully ignorant of the pain and despair all around us? I fear we are able to do this through the subtleties of selfishness disguised as holiness that tells us we must isolate ourselves, we must separate ourselves, we must 'never touch the unclean thing.' Our lives never touch, and are never touched by, the lives of the lost, broken and desperate.

How have we come to believe that living isolated from the mess, the darkness, the agony that consumes so many is to live in a place we call a *blessing?* This becomes easy for us as we buy into and spiritualized the American Dream. As long as my personal life is good as defined by the "American Dream" then I believe I am blessed.

Lord forgive us.

What did we expect when we took up our cross to follow this Savior? What did we think it would mean to be crucified with Christ? Do we believe that being a living sacrifice was meant to be a life of pleasure?

Jesus declares that a life of mourning is blessed. This blessedness comes, not so that we may avoid sorrow, but as a comforting response to our sorrow. Jesus promises that if we walk His path, embrace the sorrow and pain, *we will be comforted.* Our sorrow, our pain, our mourning are not without hope, not without purpose and we are not alone.

"Blessed are those who mourn for they will be comforted."

I am deeply convicted.

When I look in the mirror of the Word, do I not have reasons to weep over my own lack of holiness? If I weep and mourn over my lack of holiness, Christ responds with the comfort of forgiveness, cleansing and the infilling of His Spirit.

When I look upon my family, the ones over whom I am to live as a spiritual patriarch, do I not find reasons to embrace an overwhelming sorrow? If I mourn over my family, Christ responds with the assurances of his faithfulness and grace.

This happened in a very real way several months before this writing. I was begging God to be faithful to a certain family member. I do not know how God interacts with you, but it is a common occurrence for Him to interrupt my praying. He did so this time with these words: "Stop asking me to be faithful. I AM FAITHFUL: that is Who I am." I now ask that this family member would have their heart opened to see and experience the faithfulness of the Father. I am comforted as I mourn.

When I hear the stories of pain, disappointment, discouragement, despair, abuse, and hopelessness should I not be crushed? Shouldn't their pain be in my heart? Shouldn't their burdens be upon my shoulders? Shouldn't their spiritual separation from the God who loves them move me to tears? If I mourn over these stories, Christ responds with the comfort of his presence in and through my life. He might even arrange a few divine appointments so that I can be an instrument of His love and grace.

When I consider the church, do I not see reasons for deep humility and mourning? When I see the church crippled by apathy, disabled by in-fighting, and made ineffective by carelessness shouldn't I engage in desperate weeping? Empty altars, dry baptismal tanks, no testimonies of God's call to service - are these not enough to break my heart? If I mourn for the church, Christ responds with the comfort of his presence and work around, in and through the church.

I invite you to join me and plunge into mourning.

Join me in anticipating the comfort that is promised.

"Blessed are those who mourn, for they will be comforted."

Questions for reflection:

1. In what ways is value placed on the idea of happiness in our culture?

2. What value is placed on happiness in your own life?

3. When you look deeply into yourself, how is that happiness working out for you?

4. Describe a time when grief and mourning deeply impacted your life. How did you respond to that time?

5. Agree or disagree? "Mourning is one way we express our desire for grace and truth to be known." Explain your response.

6. In what way does your life or family need to feel the transforming power of grace and truth right now? Is it tear-worthy? If so, have you wept over this need?

3. MEEKNESS

Jesus succeeds in stunning the disciples and the gathered crowd: **"blessed are the poor in spirit"** and **"blessed are those who mourn."** In two short sentences Jesus makes it clear: the kingdoms of this world and the Kingdom of God are incompatible. If you and I are hearing these words as they are meant to be heard then we, too, are shocked by them.

Jesus continues without a pause: **"Blessed are the meek, for they will inherit the earth."** (vs. 5)

We must remember the historical context of this moment. The Jewish nation was living under the rule of the Roman Empire. Tiberius ruled this Empire during the time of the life, death, and resurrection of Jesus. He was haughty and cruel. Anyone who was suspected of opposition to his reign often faced execution. At his death the Empire breathed a sigh of relief.

The Jewish people longed for deliverance from exile and for centuries looked for the Messiah. They believed their Messiah would come as a great warrior to break the yoke of bondage. They looked for their Messiah to restore Israel to its strength and glory. They anticipated another Great Exodus, when God would rise up against a tyrant ruler, deliver His people with great power and glory and renew His presence among them at the newly cleansed Temple.

Anger, bitterness, hopelessness and resignation mingled in the minds of the people gathered on that hill. They wanted to be free; a dormant fire smoldered deep in their spirit just waiting for the right leader to fan that fire to new life.

And this teacher says, **"Blessed are the *meek"*?**

These listeners understood this word. They used it and heard it used to describe a person with a humble spirit who likely held the position of a servant. Meekness described a person who did not respond with hostility to any adverse circumstances. Meekness is not the message the people gathered on that hill wanted to hear. Meekness could not be a description of the leader who would bring deliverance to Israel. I imagine that some of the more zealous listeners leave about now. The message of meekness was just too much.

The message of meekness, of servitude, is still too much.

We all long to be free but have a twisted view of what it means to be free. We think we are free when we can grasp our rights, when we can sue for our rights, when we can exercise our rights – all in accordance with our political perspectives, of course – and can do so without interference. In the United States we believe that our Constitution, the Bill of Rights, and our form of government promise, provide and protect our rights and thus we are free. We are so convinced of this that we will not tolerate anything or anyone infringing on our rights.

We have marinated in this madness for so long that we believe our rights as American citizens and our rights as Christians are one and the same. We are much like the first century Jews. We, like them, long for a political/social/cultural salvation. We turn to protests, attorneys, and special action groups whenever we believe we are the victims of discrimination or persecution. We act as though we believe if our political/social/cultural rights are taken from us the church will die and we will lose our way. We have rights and those rights are both guaranteed and a guarantee. By these rights we work, buy and sell, own, and practice our faith. Without these rights nothing is *right*.

The electoral campaign of 2016 brought this into clear focus. Over and over again both sides contested for their perception of 'rights.' People sided with the particular candidate they believed best represented the preservation of those rights. Many within the church got tangled in this mess and made extreme and senseless statements. Their candidate *had* to get elected or Christianity in America was done!

God forgive us.

We believe our soldiers are serving the cause of freedom by protecting our rights. By some mysterious osmosis we believe these soldiers are also insuring our faith. We give them our greatest admiration. We say things like, "Only two people ever offered to die for your freedom: Jesus and the American soldier." We do so without thinking through the implications of such statements. Freedom achieved through war is not in any way similar to the freedom purchased by the death of Christ. Our confusion on this point is compromising our ability to speak into this post-Christian culture. I join with others in giving honor where honor is due: the men and women who serve in our military are deserving of our thanks. Even so, their service does not secure our freedom in Christ.

We curse politicians. We believe they progressively limit and infringe upon our rights. We groan in anxiety for that inevitable day when some politician will offer legislation that will make being a Christian illegal. We act like we believe politicians have the power to kill the church.

We are easily seduced by politicians. The politician will script their campaign so we are led to believe they will protect Judeo-Christian values. We jump on the bus, plant the signs, attend the rallies, engage in arguments, and scream our protests against the corrupt system. We are naïve.

We are angered when some undeserving person is given the same rights we enjoy. Our moral, ethical, and religious systems prove we deserve these rights and they do not. Simply by the fact, unchosen by us, that we were born in America proves these rights are exclusively ours.

We chafe at preachers when they have the audacity to tell us what to do. We are especially upset when we feel our rights are being challenged, even if the preacher is using Biblical principles to present that challenge. Some who are reading this may feel some of that frustration toward me right now. Please hear me anyway.

We identify our rights as blessedness. We give our civil rights a make-over so they become sacred rights as well. We shout, "God, guns and guts!" as though this trinity is an expression of cultural righteousness.

We are fighting the wrong enemy with the wrong weapons. We are fighting in the wrong war. In a moment of Divinely-induced clarity comes a sense that we shouldn't be fighting at all.

Into this chaotic noise comes the voice of the One we call Lord, confirming what we are sensing. He need not shout: the power of His voice penetrates the volume of our lives and we hear him say, **"Blessed are the meek..."**

If we hear, if for a brief moment we listen, we are unsure how to respond. We look at the ground. We shuffle our feet. We don't know what to do with our hands. We immediately formulate a response that shows we agree, all the while hoping that, somehow, our rights remain intact.

Like the gathered crowd that day, deep inside we know what **"blessed are the meek"** means. We would love to redefine the meaning of these words and Americanize their impact. We would love to blend them with our cultural context and create a more pleasing principle.

Not a chance.

Dietrich Bonhoeffer, in his book *The Cost of Discipleship,* says it like this: "...they [the meek] renounce every right of their own and live for the sake of Jesus Christ. They are determined to leave their rights to God alone... Their right is in the will of their Lord – that and no more." [5]

Citizenship in Christ's Kingdom is not about rights. Citizenship in Christ's Kingdom is about *service.* Citizenship in Christ's Kingdom is about learning to live in total subjection to Christ and the principles of His Kingdom. Citizenship in Christ's Kingdom is about living a life of service to God and service to our fellow man.

Citizenship in Christ's Kingdom is about being a servant.

Consider the words of the King of this Kingdom: **"Whoever wants to become great among you must be your servant, and whoever wants to be first must be your slave –** *just as* **the Son of Man did not come to be served, but to serve."** **(Matthew 20:27** *emphasis added*)

I see the Apostle Paul, quill in hand, pacing the floor muttering over the wording of his next paragraph. He is writing to the believers at Philippi and is searching for the

---

[5] Dietrich Bonhoeffer, *The Cost of Discipleship,* (NY, NY: Touchstone of NY, SCM Press Ltd, 1959), pg. 109. Used by permission. All rights reserved.

best way to communicate a strong truth that goes against the grain of selfishness and against the grain of personal rights. These are words that at once draw and repel even as they express a Kingdom principle. Furiously he begins to write:

> **"Your attitude should be the same that Christ Jesus had. Though he was God, he did not demand and cling to his rights as God. He made himself nothing; he took the humble position of a slave and appeared in human form. And in human form he obediently humbled himself even further by dying a criminal's death on a cross." (Philippians 2:5-8** NLT)

We are certainly thankful that Christ did as Paul has described. But...no, no, no! We will not relinquish our rights. We are *Christians!* And we live in America! We will maneuver, readjust, redefine, demand, spiritualize – whatever it takes – to find a way to have our rights and our version of a Redeemer, too.

Our hearts betray us as citizens in the kingdom of this world. We grasp at the things of this world: that is our right. We chose to forget that everyone who has ever gained anything of this world by demanding their rights will surely lose those things. One day all those things will be taken away. Jesus warns that the things of this world can be taken in a moment by a thief, corrupted by rust or eaten by a moth (see **Matthew 6**).

The earth is the inheritance of those who walk through this life as a servant, who lay no claim upon the things of this life, and who forego their rights that they might receive their reward.

The kingdom of this world makes grandiose promises which it has no power to keep. The world cannot give us what it does not own. In contrast, consider this: **"The earth is the LORD's, and everything in it, the world, and all who live in it."** **(Psalm 24:1)**

There is a day coming when the Lord will take what is His and give it to those who are His.

That is the way it works in His Kingdom.

Questions for reflection:

1. What value is placed on the idea of being a servant in our culture?

2. How do these ideas contrast with or compliment Jesus' teaching on meekness?

3. What is your definition of meekness?

4. How should we respond to the tensions between civil rights and Christian meekness?

5. What impact does the following quote have upon your life: "The earth is the inheritance of those who walk through life as a servant, who lay no claim upon the things of this life, who forego their rights that they might receive their reward"?

4. STARVING

Jesus has been speaking to his disciples – and to the eavesdropping crowd – for less than one minute. In a matter of a few seconds Jesus manages to stir the minds of these listeners in radical ways.

Poverty, mourning and servitude. These are startling words. These words create disturbing thoughts; they have the power to attract and the strength to repel. A point of decision must now be faced. The great contrast between the kingdom of this world and the Kingdom of Christ must now be acknowledged. These words give brilliant clarity to a grand truth: the kingdom of this world and the Kingdom of Christ cannot coexist within the lives of those who desire to follow Jesus.

He continues, **"Blessed are those who hunger and thirst ..."** (vs. 6)

There were those in the crowd that day, just like there are people in churches today, who interrupted their own listening with their reactive response. It would go like this: "Blessed are those who hunger and thirst – what!? So now being hungry and thirsty is a good thing, a blessed thing?"

Yielding to such a tendency we miss meaningful moments. We develop a damaging disability: listening only to react. May the Lord help us listen to learn.

This crowd knows the reality of hunger. For some, the words of Jesus are joined by the sounds of hunger, competing for attention. Few enjoy full cupboards or full stomachs. Most of them live in the constant pursuit of food. The diet of that day was simple: vegetables, fruit, and bread. Meat was a rare and expensive luxury. It was a common practice to only eat two meals a day: one at midday and another in the evening. There are at least two recorded stories of hungry crowds listening to Jesus: in each of those stories Jesus feeds them by miraculously multiplying a simple food source (see **Matthew 14** and **15**).

The people listening also know the meaning of thirst. Much of the region is dry and dusty and thirst is a constant issue.

You and I don't really understand that kind of hunger and that kind of thirst. We claim to be starving to death when we haven't eaten in a few hours, but that is because our abundance has conditioned us to eat every few hours. We claim to be so thirsty that we could spit cotton, but that is nothing compared to the potential dehydration of those who live in the arid Middle East (at www.armystudyguide.com it is recommended that each of today's soldiers deployed in the desert be given *6.5 gallons* of drinking water each day, not eight glasses a day as recommended for civilian life In the US).

These listeners are uncomfortably familiar with the issues of hunger and thirst. Jesus knows this, for he experiences the same issues as he lives among them. And still he says, **"Blessed are those who hunger and thirst…"**

His choice of words leaves little room for misunderstanding. These words are used to describe the condition of someone who is fighting to survive the onslaught of starvation, someone who is a few missed meals from death, someone weakened by hunger and thirst to the point of helplessness. These are strong words, these are contrary and disturbing words.

> "Stop drinking and see what happens. Coherent thoughts vanish, skin grows clammy, and vital organs wrinkle. Your eyes need fluid to cry; your mouth needs moisture to swallow; your glands need sweat to keep your body cool; your cells need blood to carry them; your joints need fluid to lubricate them. Deprive your soul of spiritual water, and your soul will tell you. Dehydrated hearts send desperate messages. Snarling tempers. Waves of worry. Growling mastodons of guilt and fear. You think God wants you to live with these? Hopelessness. Sleeplessness. Loneliness. Resentment. Irritability.

[6] Max Lucado, *Come Thirsty,* (Nashville, TN: Word Publishing Group, 2004), pgs. 11, 12.

Insecurity. These are warnings. Symptoms of a dryness deep within." [6]

If we choose to close our ears to these words we will miss a glorious truth.

"Blessed are those who hunger and thirst *after righteousness...*"

Oh...OK.

Jesus says we are blessed if ours is a gnawing, gut-wrenching desire for righteousness. We are blessed if we recognize that without righteousness there is no hope of survival, no hope of a full life, no hope of eternal life. Life without the relentless pursuit of righteousness is an empty existence.

Hunger for *righteousness*? How do we consume righteousness?

In our pursuit of righteousness, we create a check list of "do this and don't do that." The more exhaustive the list the more righteous we believe ourselves to be. We gather the materials for that list from tradition, unrealistic expectations of misinformed doctrine, and by using carefully selected proof texts from Scripture. Since we are fallen and broken, we start comparing and contrasting these lists of righteousness. If you have more items on your list than I have, you are a legalist. If you have fewer items on your list than I have, then you are a liberal compromiser. And my list is not fixed: I can, and will, add items at any time.

Depending, of course, on the content of the last series of revival sermons.

There have always been individuals who pursue this kind of righteousness. People who find great comfort in being right in so many obvious ways. People for whom having such a list is a source of affirmation and strength. People who are victims of their own self-will, needing control even over their righteousness.

When we live in such a way we are similar to the prodigal son who **"longed to fill his stomach with the pods that the pigs were eating..." (Luke 15:16)**. These righteousness check lists are like so much fodder. We can consume them, or be consumed by them, and yet be starving to death. Our life is not filled with satisfaction. Our life becomes filled with paranoia, discontent, and unhealthy comparisons.

Not all such people are hypocrites or self-righteous. Some are earnest followers of Jesus, wishing to live a carefully disciplined life. These people are like many of the Pharisees of Jesus' day. Jesus acknowledged that the Pharisees were righteous, but that their righteousness was incomplete (see **Matthew 5:20**).

So it is with those who pursue a check-list righteousness. Such a list can never be enough: righteousness is never found in keeping the law, whatever the source of that law.

If we give careful attention to Jesus' choice of words I believe we will discover the righteousness to which He is referring.

Some weeks prior to presenting these Beatitudes, Jesus had an encounter with a Samaritan woman. He presented her with these powerful words:

> "Everyone who drinks this water will be thirsty again, but whoever drinks the water that I give him will never thirst. Indeed, the water that I give him will become in him a spring of water welling up to eternal life." (John 4:13-14)

A few weeks after presenting the Beatitudes, Jesus has an encounter with some of the religious leaders:

> "I am the bread of life. Your forefathers ate the manna in the desert, yet they died. But here is the bread that comes down from heaven, which a man may eat and not die. I am the living bread that came down from heaven. If anyone eats of this bread, he will live forever." (John 6:48-51)

Jesus presents Himself as the only sufficient satisfaction for hunger and thirst.

Don't jump ahead of me!

The Apostle Paul wrote: **"It is because of him that you are in Christ Jesus, who has become for us wisdom from God – that is our righteousness, holiness and redemption." (1 Corinthians 1:30)**

Could it be that Jesus is saying, "Blessed are those who hunger and thirst after *Me*..."?

While you and I don't really understand hunger and thirst, we do understand the munchies. You know what I mean. We have eaten three decent meals and yet in the evening we still get the munchies. We go to the pantry and stand there looking. We finally decide on a bag of chips. Pretty good, but just doesn't do the trick. We go look in the fridge. We make a bologna sandwich with onions and spicy mustard. Close, but still not quite. To the freezer we go. Ice cream! We have the good sense to stop before we get sick, even if the munchies have not been fully satisfied.

That is an apt description of our appetite for Jesus. We mix together a little of the Gospel of John, our favorite Christian music group, and some random radio/TV preacher and an occasional Sunday School class or Sunday sermon. Just the munchies. Trying to satisfy the munchies is not the path to the promised blessing, the promised filling.

Jesus must not be an ingredient that we add to our life recipe, hoping to quiet an occasional appetite.

Watchman Nee, in his book *The Normal Christian Life,* offers these thoughts:

> "God makes it quite clear in His Word that He has only one answer to every human need: His Son, Jesus Christ. It will help us greatly, and save us from much confusion, if we keep constantly before us this fact:

God will answer all our questions in one way and one way only, namely, by showing us more of His Son." [7]

Let's paraphrase the words of Jesus this way: "Blessed are those who hunger and thirst for Me, for I am the Living Water...I am the Bread of Life...I am their righteousness. When they long after me, when they pursue me as their very life, when they are desperate for Me – *I will be all they need: in Me they will find satisfaction.*"

---

[7] Watchman Nee, *The Normal Christian Life,* (Fort Washington, PA: CLC Publishers, 2009), pgs. 9,10.

Questions for reflection:

1. In a culture saturated with extravagant sources of food and drink, describe how anyone could ever be truly hungry or thirsty.

2. How has this abundance influenced our hungering and thirsting after Christ?

3. Recount a time when the munchies filled you up but never satisfied your cravings.

4. How might the story recounted above describe your spiritual journey?

5. How is Jesus – the Living Water, the Bread of Life, and our Righteousness – to be consumed so that He becomes our continual source of satisfaction?

6. What is the role of the Lord's Supper in view of this Beatitude?

5. BEING MERCY

All who hear these teachings of Jesus are challenged by the principles of Christ's Kingdom: poor in spirit, mourning, servitude, hunger and thirst. Christ's Kingdom demands an uncompromising surrender and allegiance. This Kingdom requires that we enter it with nothing and accept, without resistance, that which the King would place upon us and expect of us.

The power of that Kingdom continues: **"Blessed are the merciful, for they will be shown mercy."** (vs. 7)

Class distinctions, oppressive taxation, relentless Romans and the Temple rules all add up to make the experience of life in first century Palestine feel less than merciful. Many common people whisper, "If I ever had the chance, I would ___" with the blank being filled with anything but acts of mercy. Others gather as like-minded resistance fighters who become known as zealots: they are intent on balancing the scales of justice by force and mercy is not part of the operational code.

And Jesus says **"Blessed are the merciful..."**

The word *merciful* is in the form of an adjective. Jesus is saying that mercy is not something we are to *do*; it is something we are to *be.* Mercy cannot be placed on a daily check list and marked off when completed. It is not a random act of kindness to be done each day as a feel-good activity. It is not a task which will ever find completion. There will never be a time when a follower of Jesus can wipe their hands and state: "Well, I'm done with that mercy thing. What's next?"

Being mercy is to live a life of active compassion. Mercy is more than external acts of pity; it is identification with the other person's situation. Mercy is laying to heart the miseries of others. Mercy moves us to drop the pretense of our personal dignity and embrace the wretchedness of those for whom Christ died. Mercy is not expressed by the "tsk, tsk" of the Levite and Pharisee as they walk by the one left for dead along the side of the road. The evidence of mercy is found on the blood-stained clothes and in the empty wallet of the Good Samaritan (see **Luke 10**).

Living as mercy is contrary. We want to cling to our rights, preserve our dignity, and protect our external reputation. We would rather live in the isolation of holy separation than risk sullying our righteous robes.

I still remember whispered conversations I overheard as a young boy. Adults would gather and begin discussing an appropriate response to someone who had sinned. They discussed the supposed merits of withdrawing from that stained person. If the good people withdrew from that marked person, it would leave no doubt about the sinfulness of the behavior in question. It was of utmost importance for the withdrawers be known and seen as uncompromising. This withdrawal must be complete: no speaking, no greeting, no relational aspects at all. The sinful person needed to receive a clear message – such behavior made them unacceptable. That poor stained saint would be left *alone*. If that person made the decision to leave that church in search for a loving congregation, the withdrawers used such action as confirmation of their worst suspicions and as affirmation of their own righteousness.

We should be eternally grateful that God did not and does not treat us in such a way. If He withdrew from us each time we sinned, had an error in judgment, or a moment of spiritual neglect we, too, would be alone. If you or I have ever been such a person as these withdrawers, *right now,* in this very moment and this very place, our hearts must cry out "Oh, Father, have mercy on me a sinner!" It would then be an appropriate Christian action to find the person against whom we have sinned and ask their forgiveness.

Late in the movie *Gladiator* there is a powerful battle scene. Maximus, played by Russell Crowe, is in a battle to the death with a previous champion gladiator, brought out of retirement for this fight. It is an intense battle. In the final moments, Maximus gains an advantage and the champion goes down. Maximus has the right as conqueror, the expectation of the crowd and the order of the Emperor to kill the fallen champion. He throws down his weapon and walks away. After a moment of disbelieving silence, someone in the vast crowd begins to chant, "Maximus the merciful.

Maximus the merciful." It is a powerful moment. Yet it falls short of the Kingdom principle of mercy. Had Maximus turned and tended the wounds of the fallen champion, had he carried him from the arena to the physicians, had he worked for and financed the champion's return to health, had he offered unconditional forgiveness to the champion for injuries received – *that would have been Kingdom mercy.*

Far too often we yield to our fallenness, like the 'withdrawers' mentioned earlier, and calibrate our compassion. We say things like, "I'm the pastor!" "I'm your mother!" "I'm _____." From that position we react and measure mercy. We say things like: "You don't know how bad you hurt me." "If you only knew what that does to me." From that perspective we determine how much compassion we will extend, if any. Other times we use our pain: if the pain is *too* deep, we will not offer any compassion or mercy. We decide the person is not worthy of mercy.

A husband reacts unkindly to his wife: "If she would just…" A parent reacts unkindly to a child: "If that boy would just…" We react unkindly to the poor: "If they would just get a job." We react unkindly to the addicted: "If they didn't make such poor decisions." We react unkindly to the morally confused living among the LGBT community: "Deluded fools. If they would just…" We react unkindly to those of a differing political perspective: "How could anyone be so stupid…" We offer the delusions that if the other person would do or be what we could approve then we would be nice to them, help them, accept them and show them mercy. We put the burden of mercy on those who need to receive it rather than on those who should simply *be it.* Mercy becomes that which is earned and, in that moment, ceases to be. And we, as citizens of the Kingdom of Christ, also cease to *be* in that moment.

Worthy of mercy? What an absurdity. Mercy is only mercy when it is unearned, when the recipient is unworthy.

Compassion and mercy are not very soluble: neither of them mixes well with selfishness, judgment, condemnation, or spiritual pride.

Consider carefully: *anytime we calibrate compassion, any time we measure mercy, at that moment we are living outside of the Kingdom of Christ.*

We are to be mercy. We must not live in the delusion that we can dispense measured mercy from our aloof place of rightness.

We must remember that we have received absurd mercy, crazy compassion. We must acknowledge we have done nothing to merit the very least of God's kindness. The only reason we have been given mercy is because of Who He is, not because of who we are or what we've done.

When – and if – we really get this, we will be compelled to extend such absurd mercy, such crazy compassion to others as a natural outflow of what we have become: *mercy*

Christ provides us with undeniable examples of being mercy.

He went into the home of a tax collector and shared a meal with other tax collectors. This act, quite contrary to the withdrawers mentioned earlier, was an act of acceptance and the beginnings of mercy.

He allows a prostitute to wash his feet with her tears and dry them with her hair. This intimate encounter bothers me: I probably would not have allowed it (too dignified, protect my reputation, etc.). Yet there it is in full color: mercy in bare feet.

When a woman was thrown at his feet, clutching a bed sheet around her, guilty of adultery, his response was living mercy. I can see him as he stoops down, takes a hand that would soon be pierced for her, and lifts her face to look into her eyes: "**Neither do I condemn you. Go, and sin no more**." Then he takes her hands in his and lifts her to her feet. Those hands then reach around and gather the sheet around her, helping hide her shame. Mercy, mercy, mercy!

He fed the hungry, by the thousands, without first asking how they could neglect to plan for lunch, without once challenging the bad decisions that placed them in a place of destitution. He just fed them.

As he walks down the street he heard this muffled groan, "Unclean! Unclean!" Rather than retreating, Jesus follows the sound, invades the personal space, and touches the leper with healing mercy. In that moment, Jesus sacrifices his ability to attend the synagogue later that day: *he* was now unclean.

Can you imagine the reputation of Jesus by this time? The story of the Gospels makes it clear. Among the religious leaders He is seen as a blasphemer, a man possessed of demons, a liar and a threat. Among the common people He is seen as one who cares, truly living out the fullness of grace and truth.

From the cross, body broken and face swollen beyond recognition, He prays forgiveness upon those who had beaten him, mocked him, and driven the spikes.

You and I acknowledge these stories. We read them. We teach them. We preach them. We give appropriate homage to the idea of mercy. And we forget. We forget Jesus is no longer here, walking among us, being mercy. We forget Jesus left His work for us to do, He left His example for us to *be.*

Even now, His mercy walks through the putrid ruins of broken lives. Wearing our shoes.

Even now, His mercy reaches out to those who are defiant and unworthy. Using our hands.

Even now, His mercy whispers into the darkness of despair. Using our voice.

Even now, His mercy seeks out the broken, the bruised, and the bitter. Using our eyes.

Even now, His mercy speaks forgiveness, peace, and hope to any and all who will hear. Using our words.

Mercy is never measured but it is messy. Mercy compels us to get involved. To touch the untouchable. To love the unlovable. To help the helpless. To embrace the broken. To speak grace to those deafened by the enemy. To carry the load. To cry the tears.

Personal cost is not part of the equation. Why? Mercy is not something we do, mercy is something we are. To not be mercy is of far greater cost.

Even now, the mercy of Christ continues to flow to us to renew what we are as we live mercy.

"Blessed are the merciful, for they will be shown mercy."

Questions for reflection:

1. Considering popular entertainment and the sense of competition in our culture, what value is placed on the giving of mercy?

2. How has the cultural perspective of mercy impacted the church?

3. How has social media influenced the expression of mercy?

4. In what ways do we tend to calibrate compassion?

5. How would you describe the mercy of God toward you?

6. In your life context, how might you be mercy? At home? At school? At work? At church?

6. CLEAN HEART: CLEAR EYES

Living in the place of God's ultimate favor, living in the blessedness of the Beatitudes, takes on a different look than the disciples and the crowd expects. They came into this moment on this mountain with learned bias. Religion, from Judaism to the pagan cultures of Rome and surrounding regions, are influences in the development of a worldview. These words of Jesus challenge those biases. These principles of the Kingdom begin the arduous process of reshaping how these listeners view the world around them and in them.

Though removed by hundreds of years, we are near neighbors of that original crowd. We, too, approach the Beatitudes with bias. That bias is informed by years of exposure to teaching and preaching. That bias is shaped by our Americanized version of Christianity. That bias might even be chained to our preferred version of the Bible.

If we allow our hearts to hear as though for the first time, we will discover that our assumptions about the Kingdom are going to be challenged and reshaped.

Poor – not more. Mourning – not happiness. Servitude – not being served. Starving – not the fatness of satisfaction. Mercy – not self-indulgence.

If I were writing a Manifesto for my kingdom it would not read like this.

Jesus continues: **"Blessed are the pure in heart, for they will see God."** (vs. 8)

Among the ancient cultures the heart represented the totality of the person. The heart was considered the center from which all life sprang. The heart was never considered as separated or disconnected from the hands, feet, mouth, ears, emotions, intentions, motives: all of life was connected to and found its source in the heart. **"Above all else, guard your heart, for it is the wellspring of life." (Proverbs 4:23)**

Jesus brought some clarity to this perspective: **"...the things that come out of the mouth come from the heart, and these make a man 'unclean.' For out of the heart come evil thoughts, murder, adultery, sexual immorality, theft, false testimony, slander."** (Matthew 15:18-19)

"The good man brings good things out of the good stored up in his heart, and the evil man brings evil things out of the evil stored up in his heart. For out of the overflow of the heart the mouth speaks." (Luke 6:45)

In our foolish delusions we separate our heart from the rest of life. We watch as someone behaves badly and respond by saying, "But they have a good heart." When someone is living in the confusion of sin and attempting to make a decision we offer this advice: "Just follow your heart," as though that is not already happening.

The principles of the Kingdom make it clear: we cannot separate our words, attitude, actions from our heart.

Every day, with every word, attitude, and action, *our heart is on display.*

We prefer to treat our heart as some separate and mystical entity, clean it up, then put it in some righteous trophy case.

We live in that tension. We feel the guilt, and rightly so, of behaving in a way that is in contrast with Kingdom principles and yet claim to have a good heart, a sanctified heart. Rather than yielding to the Voice calling to us, we redefine or redirect our choices. We hone and refine our skills at avoidance techniques. In so doing we reveal our allegiance to the kingdom of this world.

We prefer an outside–in approach.

Many years ago, while pastoring in the small town of West Blocton, Alabama, our family was blessed to be able to take a nice vacation. We made our plans, packed our bags, and jumped in the van for our week-long getaway.

As we backed out of our driveway, our refrigerator/freezer stopped working.

Words fail to describe the vile cloud that exhaled from that appliance a week later.

I am a capable person. I have learned to do a number of things around the house, including minor appliance repair. I was not intimidated by this fridge. I immediately filled a bucket with hot, soapy water and grabbed a rag. After working diligently, I stepped back and took a look. The refrigerator was squeaky clean.

Then I opened the door.

Next, I moved the unit outside and positioned it over a tarp. I went to the shed and got out my compressor and paint gun. The local hardware store provided the necessary appliance paint. A few hours later that appliance looked like new.

Then I opened the door.

Not willing to admit defeat, I decided the fridge needed a new location: maybe the other appliances were preventing it from recovering. I moved it to another room, even making it the centerpiece of the room.

Did not help.

By now you have decided that I am the one who needs help.

Haven't we all handled life with this outside–in approach? We indulge in retail therapy in hopes that a new wardrobe will make us a new person. We change our style in search of a new me. We join the local gym, in the hope of shedding a few pounds and being lifted to a new life. We decide to hang out with a better class of friends. Some of us even decide to find a cooler church.

Then grace interrupts and opens the door to our inner life.

Yuck. Still stinks.

Jesus declares a new life starts and ends with the heart.

The heart must be made clean. We must allow the work of
the Spirit to bring us into the blessedness of being genuine,
clean, with no presence of falsehood. Such a life, changed
from the inside, is described this way: **"...love, joy, peace,
patience, kindness, goodness, faithfulness, gentleness, and
self-control." (Galatians 5:22-23)**

We are no more able to cleanse our own heart than the
above-mentioned refrigerator could cleanse itself. We try so
hard to do better. We cry out for the strength to be better.
The attempt to self-cleanse the heart becomes a life-long
struggle. All to no avail. God is simply not going to allow a
dirty us to become the cleaning agent for ourselves. This is a
work to which we must yield without reserve. God is the
only One qualified and capable to cleanse us from within. He
does this, not by enhancing our efforts, but by the finished
work of Christ.

When the heart is cleansed, all of life is now an expression of
that cleansing.

Remember – *our life is our heart on display*.

There is a great promise to those whose heart is pure: **"they
will see God."**

Only those whose heart is cleansed by the presence of Christ and His Word, whose lives are clean, *will see God.*

I am unwilling to lose the power of this promise by relegating it to some eschatological definition. Jesus is speaking to the right-here, right-now crowd.

I am bothered by the right-here, right-now reality of this truth. If I could relegate seeing God to a later time and a different place, I can leave the truth of cleansing detached from my life, at least for today. If this truth is to be received as a right-now, right-here truth then I am forced to deal with it.

We all want to see God. We testify to it. We pray for it. We long to see God move, act, answer. In contrast to this longing to see God, we speak as though God is handicapped by the godless culture of our nation, by the dysfunctions within the church, and by the collapse of morals in our families.

"Blessed are the pure in heart, for they will see God."

God is at work. He is on the job. He is present. If we don't see Him it is not because He is not to be seen. Could it be that we *cannot see*? Could it be that an impure heart, and by extension a poorly lived life, is blinding our eyes to the reality of the presence and work of the Living God?

I want to see Him! Not only a thousand years from now but today, right now, right here.

Do I dare believe that such a thing is possible? Do I dare embrace this radical Kingdom principle of the connection between cleansing and clarity?

Yes, yes, yes!

"Lord cleanse me now!"

Questions for reflection:

1. How does our culture view the human heart? The human condition?

2. How has that perspective influenced the teachings of the church?

3. In what ways is there a contrast between your own behavior and who you declare yourself to be?

4. How have you attempted to resolve that contrast? Has it worked?

5. In what areas of life do you wish to see God?

6. How would you respond to this statement: "Cleansing and clarity are inseparably connected."? Why that response?

7. BEING PEACE

Those who were listening to Jesus on that day desired peace. The Jewish listeners expressed that desire with the word "shalom." This greeting was given and received; it gave voice to their desire for personal and national well-being. The Greek listeners wanted peace as the cessation of war. The governor of the region, assigned by the Romans, was tasked with keeping peace, a fragile reality indicated in more than one Gospel account.

Jesus speaks to the issue of peace. He does not envision peace as a condition provided by some superior force or by the signing of a treaty, but rather as a matter of personal behavior: **"Blessed are the peacemakers, for they will be called the sons of God."** (vs. 9). The language of Jesus makes peace the responsibility of each individual. Imagine being a first century listener and hearing these words through your own cultural bias. Someone else – emperor, messiah, military general – is to be the instrument of peace. No commoner has any hope of making any significant difference in bringing about peace. Hearing this Teacher state that peace is not an action to be done but rather a way to *be* must have been startling. This man states that at all places and at all times, among any people or circumstance, *we are to be peace.*

Each person is to bring about peace, perform acts of peace, to do what makes for peace. Each person is to be an active agent of peace. Not as a thing to do but as the natural outflow of what that person *is*.

Impossible.

I remember playing "King of the Mountain" when I was a boy. You know the game. Any high spot would do: a pile of rocks, a mound of dirt or wood shavings. Some kid climbs to the top, throws out his arms and declares, "I am King of the mountain!" That declaration is not heard as an announcement; it is heard as a challenge. A battle ensues. Pushing, shoving, tripping, punching – any act of violence is attempted to remove that "king" and take his place.

Harmless enough when you're nine.

Not so much when you're an adult.

Yes, we still play "King of the Mountain." It goes by a much more adult title: *power struggle.*

We know that game well. It is a cultural brand, a tattoo of strength: "I have power and you do not." Watch some reality show. What you see there is a constant and vicious battle for power, control and the #1 spot.

This power struggle is not only an ugly reality in some scripted TV show. The ugliness of this struggle is seen in personal relationships. Husband and wife pitted against one another. Parents and teens locked in constant struggles. Siblings fighting over scraps of inheritance. Neighbors bickering over a property line.

Our communities are divided as we battle for power.

As a Town Councilman I saw this first hand as we wrestled with the issue of allowing Walmart to come to our small town. No fists were thrown but words were. Strong opinions were expressed in accusatory tones. A small, but vocal, minority wanted to displace Council members in the upcoming Council elections. I credit our Mayor with tempering the tempers with these words: "We were neighbors before this discussion and will be neighbors after. Let's remember that." He was a peacemaker in a tense time.

It pains me to acknowledge the ugliness of power struggles is not confined to the world. The struggle for power is an ugliness on exhibition in many churches. The individual who challenges church election results – only when the nominations or elections do not go as desired by that individual. The board member who believes he has the right to control every detail of the pastor's life. The disgruntled member who consistently reads negative motives into every spoken, or unspoken, word. The pastor who is easily threatened by any attempt to question decisions or to offer appropriate accountability. The family that reminds church leadership about the amount of money they have given to the church. The pastor who reminds the church of the difficulties of being a pastor...of being *their* pastor. Each one building a mountain upon which they place themselves as king.

These power plays are not only in the church; the church uses them against the world. As a pastor I receive a constant flow of mail urging me to lead my congregation to join thousands of others in the fight for religious freedom. The tone of most of these letters (the ones I bother to read) goes something like this: some anti-church entity or group is going to take our freedom away so those on the religious right need to work hard to gather more money, have bigger rallies, and shout louder. Then there are usually several select events, edited to fit the need, that prove their point. On my desk at this very moment is such a mailing. These mailings are riddled with fear, with labeling, and with creating a common enemy where such an enemy may not exist.

I've lived long enough and watched closely enough to state with some conviction: such an approach has not and will not work. Dan Boone, President of Trevecca Nazarene University, addresses this in his excellent book *A Charitable Discourse: Talking About the Things That Divide Us:*

> "The theology of holy love has as much to lose from a divisive, arrogant spirit as from the positions we end up with. It may be that we win the verbal spar, the war of castigation, the battle for minds, the political election – and lose the peace that characterizes Christ. And while we duke it out, a generation has

left the church in hopes of finding an honest, mature conversation to join. This reality has become the call of my life – to live among young thinkers in hopes of instilling a way of conversing that honors God, deals with life, is shaped by Scripture, and forms a generation of holy leaders who have the courage to live and think like the kingdom – people of God rather than the people of the kingdoms of this world." [8]

We have been seduced to believe that we can achieve our definition of peace by using the methods of the world, looking for someone or something else to be our champion. When a leader arises within the evangelical right and grandstands on the right issues we will carry him on our shoulders as our hero. When a smooth-talking politician uses carefully scripted language and makes carefully chosen promises we place our hopes on them and place their poster in our front yard. We are quick to sacrifice peace for the sake of winning the culture war.

By our nature we resort to power plays. When confronted, our first response is to grasp for power to defend ourselves.

---

[8] Dan Boone, *A Charitable Discourse: talking about the things that divide us,* (Kansas City, MO: Beacon Hill Press of Kansas City, 2010), pg. 137. Used by permission. All rights reserved.

When overlooked, we manipulate power to expose this injustice. When disappointed, misused or sense injustice, we start to play the adult version of "King of the Mountain." In so doing we leave a trail of debris: anger, disappointment, frustration, confusion, sadness and a destroyed testimony.

I have seen this first hand. A Christian was behaving badly by expressing a horrible attitude, spreading angry demands to everyone around them, being chronically negative and hyper-critical. When given a firm-grace confrontation their attack against me was quick, angry, and cruel.

Jesus would have us *be peace.* Here is the difficulty with this expectation: we cannot be peace if we are not at peace. Holding on to past hurts not only keeps that wound open but also gives us a fleshly sensitivity: from that sensitivity we often lash out and cause hurt. When we continue to see ourselves as victims we will often act as a victimizer. If we do not allow the memories of our own sinfulness to fade through grace, we will lose our ability to focus on Christ through faith. Forgiveness, daily grace, and the continuing work of the Holy Spirit are enough to help us release the past and be at peace.

At the birth of this One we call Savior, angels sang a hymn of peace (**Luke 2:14**). This One we call Savior gives the gift of His peace to those who follow Him (**John 14:27**). The Apostle Paul declares this One we call Savior to be our peace (**Ephesians 2:14**). Once the Holy Spirit fills a believer, that Spirit produces peace in and through that life (**Galatians**

5:22). That same Spirit inspired these words to be written: **"Make every effort to live in peace with all men and be holy: without holiness no one will see the Lord." (Hebrews 12:14)**

James declares: **"The wisdom that comes from heaven is first of all pure: then peace-loving… Peacemakers who sow in peace raise a harvest of righteousness." (3:17-18)**

In the midst of inter-personal relationships within the church we are called to **"make every effort to do what leads to peace and to mutual edification." (Romans 14:19).**

While our attempts at being peace may not always bring peace, we are never given permission to be troublemakers:

> **"You, my brothers, were called to be free. But do not use your freedom to indulge the sinful nature; rather, serve one another in love. The entire law is summed up in a single command: 'Love your neighbor as yourself.' If you keep on biting and devouring each other, watch out or you will be destroyed by each other." (Galatians 5:13-15)**

Rather than demanding our rights, rather than making sure everybody knows we are right, why don't we *get right*? **"May God himself, the God of peace, sanctify you through and through." (1 Thessalonians 5:23)**

Rather than stomping through this life as a troublemaker, why don't we walk in peace, having our **"feet fitted with the**

readiness that comes from the gospel of peace" (Ephesians 6:15)?

Rather than filling our safes with guns in anxious preparation for a confrontation, why don't we fill our heart, head, and mouth with the message of peace?

Isn't the promise to the peacemaker worth the effort? **"...they will be called the children of God."**

I have been in several settings where an ID tag was required. I was given a lanyard with my picture ID hanging on the end. Or I was given a peel-and-stick name tag. The ID tags allowed someone to know my name. The ID tag did not allow them to know *me*. The ID told them nothing of my heritage, my family, or my character.

The promise to peacemakers is much deeper and more meaningful than some name tag or ID card.

This promise means that those who are peace will carry upon them the very name and the very nature of God. Not their own name, not their own nature. His.

Living as a troublemaker only exposes who, what and whose we are.

Living as peace declares who and what God is.

Those who claim the name of God and yet live as troublemakers are in danger of taking the Lord's name in vain by their very life.

Those who are peace honor the name of the Lord who is peace; they show the world the very nature of the One we call Savior.

We need peace. Our families need peace. Our communities need peace. Our churches need peace.

And we are called to *be peace*. In our families. In our communities. In our schools. In our churches.

That is the way it works in His Kingdom.

Questions for reflection:

1. In what ways is peace being challenged in our culture?

2. How is this culture influencing the church's view of peace?

3. It what ways has your own behavior been in contrast to peace?

4. Are you at peace with the sins, events, and people of your own past?

5. Respond to this statement: "Without the cleansing effect of grace, time does not make past injuries better but rather only makes them bitter."

6. Christ is the author of peace. In what ways does He need to work that peace in your life right now?

8. PERSECUTED

I am profoundly convicted and challenged by the words of Jesus: less of me, deep mourning, servitude, starvation hunger for Him, being mercy and being peace. The more I look into His Word, the more intensely I listen to His voice, the more I am aware of my own overwhelming need for holiness. I trust you feel the same.

This conviction does not grow any less with these words of Jesus:

> **"Blessed are those who are persecuted because of righteousness, for theirs is the kingdom of heaven. Blessed are you when people insult you, persecute you and falsely say all kinds of evil against you because of me. Rejoice and be glad, because great is your reward in heaven, for in the same way they persecuted the prophets who were before you."**
> (vss. 10-12)

That is not the spin most American Christians apply to persecution and suffering. We have a rather odd definition of persecution. This odd definition has been made quite clear in the past few years. Phil Robertson, the preacher-dad of *Duck Dynasty* aired on *A&E,* made some strong statements in an interview. Those statements caused *A&E* to consider action against him and against the show. All over America

Christians began screaming about losing their freedom of speech. Was this persecution? Not hardly.

Not long ago a county clerk in Kentucky, Kim Davis, was jailed for refusing to obey a court order to issue same-sex marriage licenses. Christians all over America began crying about persecution. Was this persecution? Not hardly.

Let's be honest. Freedom of speech and freedom from the consequences of speech are two entirely different things. Let's be honest again: freedom to exercise religious beliefs and freedom from the consequences of those beliefs is also two entirely different things.

We, the American Christians, have come to define any momentary inconvenience or setback as persecution. How can we define something as persecution when we still have the power to hire an attorney and take legal action? How can we define something as persecution when we can write a best-selling book about our experience, go on book-signing tours, become a national celebrity, make the national talk shows, and be paraded out on numerous special interest platforms?

That does not sound like persecution to me. Sounds more like *opportunity*...

Consider the words of John McArthur:

> "The atmosphere surrounding today's evangelical church, with its emphasis on easy believism and 'feel-

good-about-yourself' Christianity, has fostered an unbiblical attitude among believers toward the existence of suffering and persecution in their lives. In addition to the natural aversion to pain and difficulty, many Christians have acquired the notion that hardships should not even cross their paths." [9]

We find a clear definition of persecution in the Bible:

> **"Others were tortured and refused to be released, so that they might gain a better resurrection. Some faced jeers and flogging, while still others were chained and put in prison. They were stoned; they were sawn in two; they were put to death by the sword. They went about in sheepskins and goatskins, destitute, persecuted, and mistreated – the world was not worthy of them. They wandered in deserts and mountains, and in caves and holes in the ground." (Hebrews 11:36-38)**

Jesus declares that these believers lived in blessedness.

Not sure I like that.

Peter, the Apostle who suffered persecution and was executed for his faith, wrote:

---

[9] John McArthur, *The Power of Suffering*, (Wheaton, IL: Victor Books, 1995), from the introduction.

"Dear friends, don't be surprised at the fiery trials you are going through, as if something strange were happening to you. Instead, be very glad – because these trials will make you partners with Christ in his sufferings, and afterward you will have the wonderful joy of sharing his glory when it is displayed to all the world. Be happy if you are insulted for being a Christian, for then the glorious Spirit of God will come upon you. If you suffer, however, it must not be for murder, stealing, making trouble, or prying into other people's affairs. But it is no shame to suffer for being a Christian. Praise God for the privilege of being called by his wonderful name!" (1 Peter 4:12-16 NLT)

Jesus speaks of persecution and opposition, not as something that naturally comes to us as a result of our poor choices, but as a result of righteousness. As we noted in reference to an earlier Beatitude (**"Blessed are those who hunger and thirst after righteousness…."**), Christ is our righteousness. In this Beatitude about persecution, Jesus joins **"because of righteousness"** and **"because of me"** as the cause for such persecution and opposition. When we live out Christ in the public and private arenas of life we can expect those of the kingdom of the world to hate us as they hated – and still hate – Him. Hatred is never expressed in ways that bring peace, comfort, or inclusion. Hatred always expresses itself in some form of violence against that which is hated.

Jesus says that when such a thing happens we are to rejoice and be glad. The phrase **"rejoice and be glad"** is an interesting phrase. This phrase indicates a condition of being overjoyed, of being filled with exuberance, of shouting for joy. We hear these words of Jesus, smile and utter some folk theology: "Oh, of course he does not mean to rejoice about being persecuted. He means we can rejoice in spite of being persecuted."

Really?

> **"They** (the Sanhedrin) **called the apostles in and had them flogged. Then they ordered them not to speak in the name of Jesus, and let them go. The apostles left the Sanhedrin,** *rejoicing because they had been counted worthy of suffering disgrace for the Name.* **Day after day, in the temple courts and from house to house, they never stopped teaching and proclaiming the good news that Jesus is the Christ."** (**Acts 5:40-42** emphasis added).

Our responses during supposed persecutions are contrary to this Beatitude and this story from the early church. We whine, cry, hire attorneys, visit national talk shows, sign book deals, and organize rallies. Let me retell the above story as though it happened in 21st century America –

> After being arrested, the Christians stood before a judge who ordered them placed in county lockup for the next thirty days. After serving their sentence,

they were released with a stern warning. As these Christians walked out into the sunlight, they were greeted by hundreds of supporters carrying protest banners: "Free the Christians!" With upraised hands symbolizing victory, these Christians approached a bank of microphones set up for this occasion. Once the TV camera lights blink on, one Christian announces pending legal action, another announces a book deal already in the works, a third announces receiving an invitation to join a political candidate's campaign, and yet another announces the date when they would be the key note speaker at a large rally. All these announcements were met with shouts of support.

Does that sound like what Jesus taught and how the first century Christians responded to persecution?

Words from Bishop J. C. Ryle seem fitting here:

> "A man...must be content to be thought ill of by man if he pleases God. He must count it no strange thing to be mocked, ridiculed, slandered, persecuted and even hated. He must submit to be thought by many a fool...to have his words perverted and his actions misrepresented. In fact, he must not marvel if some call him mad. The Master says – 'Remember the word that I said to you, The servant is not greater than his lord. If they have persecuted me, they will also persecute you; ...' (John 15:20) It is always

unpleasant to be spoken against and forsaken and lied about and to stand alone. But there is no help for it. The cup which our Master drank must be drunk by his disciples. To be a Christian will cost a man the favor of the world." [10]

Jesus provides two points of evidence that should enable our rejoicing and gladness: **"great is your reward in heaven"** and **"in the same way they persecuted the prophets who were before you."**

We cannot embrace these points of evidence if we live in the shortsightedness of our Americanized version of Christianity. We must learn to take the long view and discern our place in that view.

We must learn the long view forward and upward. Heaven is the source of our reward. This is the theme Jesus revisits when teaching on giving, prayer, and fasting (**Matthew 6**). Far too often we are distracted by the rewards of men: legal judgments in our favor, book deals, and becoming a Christian celebrity. These words of Jesus apply in such cases: **"I tell you the truth, they have received their reward in full."** (**Matthew 6:2, 5, 16**)

We must learn that our reward comes from the Father who is in heaven. His smile. His applause. His strength. His manifested presence.

---

[10] J.C. Ryle, *Holiness: Its Nature, Hindrances, Difficulties and Roots*, (Cambridge, UK: Cambridge University Press, 1959), pg. 71.

We must learn that heaven holds our future reward: **"I consider that our present sufferings are not worth comparing with the glory that will be revealed in us."** **(Romans 8:18)**

We must also learn to take a long view backward. In so doing, we discover there is a long list of God's children who have suffered. Those who suffer because of Christ are in really good company! The writer to the Hebrews reminds us that the world was not worthy of such individuals (**Hebrews 11:38**). There must be no pride for our inclusion in such a list, only rejoicing and gladness to the glory of God.

Less of me, deep mourning, servitude, starvation for Jesus, being mercy, being peace, and rejoicing because of persecution – that is the way it works in Christ's Kingdom.

And according to Jesus that describes a blessed life.

Questions for reflection:

1. How does our culture view the idea of being mistreated?

2. How has this cultural idea invaded the American church?

3. How is the American Christian's view of persecution in contrast with much of the rest of Christians in the world? With the Bible?

4. Respond to this statement by John McArthur: "...the key to being like Christ in the midst of suffering and persecution is to be like Him at all other times." (*The Power of Suffering,* pg. 12)

9. THE INVASION

The culture of Jesus' day had no problem with individuals embracing various forms or practices of religion, so long as those practices remained personal and private. In the life of the early church as recorded in the book of **Acts**, the followers of Jesus did not get into trouble because they followed Jesus: they were in trouble because following Jesus was having a public impact. This movement was seen as a religious and political threat and great efforts were made to extinguish the Christ followers.

Had these earliest Christians decided to make following Jesus a private matter to be practiced in secret, no doubt the story recorded in the book of **Acts** would not be as we know it today.

Most societies are tolerant of that which remains in the shadows. We express that tolerance like this: "Why should I care what people do in their private life?" "Why should you care? I'm not hurting anyone." "Who are we to dictate what people do in their own bedrooms?" Anytime these private issues are thrust into the public spot light, suddenly we do care. When our sense of values is challenged or violated, when our sense of safety is shaken, when the comfortable routine is rerouted – then we care.

When private gun ownership becomes public violence. When deviant sexuality headlines the news. When private religion gets a public platform. When...and suddenly we are embroiled in controversy. The pretense of tolerance is shattered.

Jesus had completed describing the character of those in His Kingdom. I believe Jesus was being purposeful in putting persecution as the final Beatitude: *live like this and you will get in trouble.* From that final Beatitude we are getting a first glimpse into a disturbing reality: following Jesus as a citizen of His Kingdom, yet living in this world, will create tension and trouble.

> "It is not difficult to understand why a church would want to disconnect from the world around it. Just watching the five o'clock news can make a person want to give up. If our perception is that people don't care anyway, if our conclusion is that no one is really open to the truth, and since there's overwhelming evidence that the hearts of individuals and the heart of society seems to have hardened beyond repair, it is no wonder that churches have become spiritual bomb shelters. Yet the church is not called to survive history but to serve humanity"[11]

---

[11] Erwin Raphael McManus, *An Unstoppable Force,*(Loveland, CO: Group Publishing Inc., 2001), pg. 23.

The teachings of Jesus confront us with this truth: there is no way for a follower of Jesus to be unseen and unheard, to live as "out of sight, out of mind."

Jesus is saying, "I have described to you the character of a citizen in my Kingdom. Now let me show you how that citizen will impact the world."

Inevitable. Unavoidable.

This is how a citizen of the Kingdom is meant to be.

10. SALT

"You are the salt of the earth. But if the salt loses its saltiness, how can it be made salty again? It is no longer good for anything, except to be thrown out and trampled by men." (vs. 13)

We make a mistake if our thoughts go immediately to the iodized salt that can be purchased for reasonable cost at the local grocery store: that salt has been processed in ways unknown in the days of Jesus.

Salt has been in use since the beginning of civilization and is referenced in some of the oldest historical records. Salt was used for the preservation of food, as currency when purchasing a slave (from that practice we get the phrase "not worth his salt") and as payment for services rendered (from this practice we get our word "salary"). It was a common component in religious rituals, symbolizing the steadfastness of the covenant relationship between the people and their god.

The salt of Jesus' day and location was gathered from the Dead Sea by the process of natural evaporation. What remained was a corrupted salt with a limited shelf life. The corruptions within the salt became evident as the salt lost its saltiness.

When Jesus says, **"You are the salt of the earth"**, these first listeners immediately thought in practical terms.

As should we.

Jesus presents this not as something to do but as something we are. Being salty is not offered as one of several options. Being salty is not on a multiple-choice check list, not on some spiritual gifts discovery chart. Jesus never offers an aptitude test to enable the people to discover and best apply their saltiness.

Salt is what we are as citizens in Christ's Kingdom living in this world.

What does this mean? How are we to understand this existence?

Among the ancient people, salt's greatest use was its ability to preserve. Without artificial means of food preservation, salt was invaluable in its ability to preserve food which would then be stocked for future use. Survival often depended on the power of salt.

In order for salt to do its work it had to be applied and allowed to penetrate the food product.

As followers of Jesus, living out the Beatitudes, we are to be in the world. Our very presence in society is meant to slow the corruption that is all around us.

I am saddened each time I hear someone make a prayer request like this: "Pray that I get a different job. I'm the only Christian in my department and it is so hard. I'm praying for a job among good Christian people." If we reinterpret that request in light of being salt: "Pray that I don't have to be salt anymore. I'm the only salty person in my department. Why do I have to be the one? Why do I have to be responsible for slowing or stopping the corruption in that place?"

How about this one: "Pray that our house will sell. We just can't live by those neighbors anymore. They drink, cuss, and behave in embarrassing ways around their pool. We need to get into a good neighborhood." Let's reinterpret that prayer in light of being salt...

You get the point: as followers of Jesus we are an invasive force meant to bring radical change to our world.

Our culture is increasingly corrupt. It seems that corruption is gaining momentum at an astonishing rate. We are no longer shocked when we hear yet another report of godless behavior. Consider this quote from Arthur Custance:

> "The race is not a series of whole Adams, but the fragments of a single Adam. Together we thus constitute the body of Adam, an entity as real and as articulate as the Body of Christ. Were it not for the existence of the Body of Christ, this other diseased body would soon manifest itself for what it is,

without restraint. Here we have the basis of our Lord's statement, 'Ye are the salt of the earth.'" [12]

Our responses to reports or experiences of corruption are predicable. We make minimal effort to confirm the report (especially if it fits into our social/political bias) before we share the news. We will find someone to blame. We will blame it on the politicians. We will blame it on the homosexual community. We will blame it on the public school system. We will blame it on the flood of immigrants. We will blame it on cell phones, video games, TV, popular music and movies, bad parenting, the welfare system, President Obama, President Trump – anything and anybody other than the church (well, *our church,* anyway).

Here is the real problem: followers of Jesus have drifted away from living out the Beatitudes in the world and as a consequence we have lost our saltiness. As a result, by the words of Jesus, **"It is no longer good for anything, except to be thrown out and trampled by men."**

It is *not* salty behavior to join up with like-minded people and carry protest banners, to shout louder, to create and support political action committees, to resort to name calling, to craft

---

[12] Arthur Custance, *Man In Adam and In Christ,* The Doorway Papers, volume three, (Grand Rapids, MI: The Zondervan Corporation, 1975), pgs. 183-4. Emphasis is the author's.

our skill at creating a common enemy we all can hate, to put labels on everybody with whom we disagree, and to stoke the fires of fear. What happens in most of these situations is best described by this illustration:

When I was in college a few students thought it was funny to loosen the lid to the salt shakers that were found on each table in the cafeteria. When the next person used that salt shaker the entire contents poured out on their food and made it distasteful beyond eating.

A concentration of salt in one small area makes for a distasteful situation. It actually has the opposite effect of that which is intended. Rather than scattering and preserving, concentrated salt actually repels.

The church has been trying this for years. I have lived long enough and paid enough attention to say this: *It has not worked.*

It *will not work.*

When we engage the world with the world's own methods, we introduce a corrupting agent into the salt and it loses its saltiness. We gather crowds, make grandstand pronouncements, create a 501(c)3 and receive a flood of donations, but we are not be salt.

The only thing that will cause salt to lose its saltiness is the presence of impurities. Any time we imitate the ways of this world, we introduce an impurity. Any time we reach into the kingdom of this world for moral definitions, we introduce an impurity. Any time we reach into the kingdom of this world and gather weapons, we introduce an impurity.

And we lose our saltiness.

Jesus states we impact our world as salt or we serve no purpose at all. This is a powerful, fearful, and offensive statement. The religious influences in my early life told me I must flee the world and seclude myself away from all worldly influences. This influence sent an unspoken message that declared Christianity as too fragile to survive interacting with the world. This teaching of Jesus gives the opposite message: my followers, living as salt, have the power to change the world.

Salty behavior is seen when there is a decrease of selfishness (poor in spirit), brokenness (mourning), servitude (meekness), hunger and thirst for Jesus, being mercy, being peace, and rejoicing in opposition.

We must live out the Beatitudes *in the world*. On the job. In the class room. On the ball field. On the highway. In the check-out line. Interacting with customer service. During disagreeable conversations. In family relationships. Even with the telemarketer.

Our presence, our invasion into the world as salt, is to be a preserving presence. We are those who slow the growth of corruption by our living influence.

One other aspect of salt is its use in religious rituals to show the strength of covenant between the people and their god.

The people of Israel were to include salt in all their grain offerings (**Leviticus 2:13**). The phrase "**covenant of salt**" is used at least three times in describing relationship between God and His people (**Leviticus 2:13; Numbers 18:19; 2 Chronicles 13:5**). The use of salt was a continual reminder of the covenantal relationship between Israel and the One True God.

Our presence in this world as salt is a constant reminder of the covenantal relationship God desires to have with all people. God is the architect and the guarantor of this covenant. Christ came as the Word (see **John 1**) and has declared the terms of this covenant. This covenant is founded upon the finished work of Christ and is available to all who will accept the work of Christ on their behalf.

We are in the world as the living document of this covenant. Even our words are to be influenced by this covenant: **"Let your conversation be always full of grace, *seasoned with salt*, so that you may know how to answer everyone."** (**Colossians 4:6** *emphasis added*)

We are the living, walking, speaking invasion of the preserving covenant of the One True God.

This mandate of Jesus is convicting, challenging, and contrary to our nature.

It is impossible without Him.

Questions for reflection:

1. What evidence have you observed that our culture is becoming increasingly corrupt?

2. By your observations, what is being done about this corruption? Who is leading the challenge? What effect is this having?

3. What corruption exists in your life context? Work, school, community, etc.

4. What is being done to address these areas of corruption?

5. What difference would you, being salt, make in each of these situations?

11. LIGHT

Jesus did not present the Beatitudes as character traits to be developed in private and lived out in secret. The Beatitudes are to have a transforming effect on and in us and then have a transforming effect through us.

Jesus states that as a result of the Beatitudes we invade the world as salt, slowing the rate of corruption where we live and work, being the living document of the covenantal relationship God desires to have with all people. Now he states we are to penetrate the darkness of our world as light:

> **"You are the light of the world. A city on a hill cannot be hidden. Neither do people light a lamp and put it under a bowl. Instead they put it on its stand, and it gives light to everyone in the house. In the same way, let your light shine before men, that they may see your good deeds and praise your Father in heaven."** (vss. 14-16)

As we consider his words we must put them in the context of the early first century listener. Those listeners had a limited knowledge of light. It is unlikely that they had extensive knowledge of light spectrums, light waves, or the speed of light. They did not have advanced equipment by which they could take measurements and study the properties of light. They certainly had no concept of artificial light sources. Their understanding of light was limited to the observation of the sun, moon, stars, and fire. If we choose to use today's knowledge of light – spectrums, light absorption and reflection to create color, waves, speed, and 'bendability' – we will be distracted from the simple yet profound truth intended.

Jesus narrows their thinking to flame, particularly the flame of a lamp.

For a few moments let's simplify our thinking and take a seat among that first century crowd.

What might they interpret these words of Jesus to mean? What truth would they draw from their lamps that would impact how they would live life?

They would notice Jesus did not offer them a lamp, literal or metaphorical, that they would then use to light their world. He is making no suggestions on how to create an instrument of light. He is not implying in any way that light be added to some kind of life arsenal.

He is declaring **"You *are* the light of the world."**

If I am to think of *me* as being light like the flame of a simple oil lamp, what does that mean?

It means that I am not the source, or fuel, of the flame. The flame and its source are not the same thing. So that immediately begs a question: what is the source, or fuel, of me being light?

Oil. Olive oil. That is the source in the lamp at home (first century, remember?).

The thinking process might have taken a journey something like this -

"Oil...olive oil. Among our ancestors such oil was used in the lamps of the tabernacle and Temple. It was also used for anointing priests and kings, even prophets. On more than one occasion such anointing caused the Spirit of God to come upon that priest, king or prophet. Hmmm. Could this teacher be telling us that we need the Spirit of God to come upon us as the source of our being light in the world? In some mystical way, is our body meant to be the vessel in which this Spirit of God dwells as our source? How do we replenish this Spirit so our fire does not go out?"

The light of a fire is never its own source. Fire never simply exists. Fire is completely dependent upon an immediate and uninterrupted connection with its fuel source. There is a cause and effect cycle: fuel, fire, light. Remove the fuel there is no fire; remove the fire there is no light. We know this to be true in the law of physics, yet do we know this truth in the realm of our spiritual journey?

Could this explain the confusion and compromise that are evident among those who claim the name of Christ? If we attempt to be light without fuel and fire we are living in a religious delusion. From that place of delusion it doesn't take long for our opinions, biases, and prejudices to be the fuel of anger, division, and condemnation. A great deal of heat is generated but no light.

I can't help but think of two very different types of oxidation. I will not bore you with a lesson in chemical reactions to explain oxidation but know this: both fire and rust are forms of oxidation. One form of oxidation provides light and heat; the other corrupts and brings ruin (Jesus acknowledged the destructive power of rust: **Matthew 6:19**). Is any further comment needed?

What else might we learn about being light?

Light is obvious. Light is different from everything else and is always in contrast to the darkness. Light can be seen from a distance and is not mistaken for something else when viewed up close. There is no debate: it is light. When outside at the campfire, it is light. When inside flickering from a wick, it is light.

There is a constancy about light. Its nature is so fixed that it cannot exist as something else. Flame never gives a false light in this place and a true light in that place. The identity of light and darkness are never confused.

When living out the Beatitudes our lives will be obviously different than the darkness. We won't be one way in this place and a contrasting way in that place. While we must go into the darkness – that is where light is most obvious – we will not suddenly be part of that darkness. The nature of light does not permit for public shining and private darkness. Not ever.

Jesus help us.

Jesus tells these listeners light is always purposeful: **"neither do people light a lamp and put   it under a bowl. Instead they put it on its stand, and it gives light to everyone in the house."**

Light has a purpose: a simple, profound, beautiful purpose – *shine*.

Since the working presence of the Beatitudes in us *makes us light*, we have a simple, profound, and beautiful purpose: *shine*.

We do not have the option to turn the light on or off to suit our situation. We cannot turn the light on at work and then off at home so we can relax. We cannot turn the light on at church so we can worship and then turn it off we when go to school Monday morning. We cannot turn it on when talking with colleagues then turn it off for our private hobby.

We will shine everywhere, among any people, all the time. Everyone we encounter is to be affected by us as light. No exceptions, no discrimination.

The very nature of light is to shine.

I know that being a follower of Jesus is a personal matter. I can't follow Him for you and your following Him is not credited to my account. A relationship with Jesus is personal. Following Jesus also makes us light and as such it cannot be private. As light it is impossible for us to hide. A light that does not shine is inconceivable.

Years ago our daughter took an interest in oil lamps. We bought her quite an interesting collection across a few years. They were oil lamps by definition and design. No one would argue that identification. Yet they were not really lamps until they were fueled and lit. Until fueled and lit they were lamps in name only.

Jesus makes a bit of an issue of this point: **"In the same way** (as a lamp is put on its stand to give light to everyone in the house) **let your light shine before men, that they may see your good deeds and praise your Father in heaven."**

Let's just say it: anybody can do good deeds.

Let's just say it: not all good deeds give glory to God.

Some do good deeds to build a reputation or to inflate their personal resume. While the deed is good, the motive is selfish and evil. There is no light in such action.

The deed done is not the light; the one doing the deed is the light.

That life shines so the motivation behind the good deed is seen by all – no grand announcement necessary. No applause is sought. No attention is required. No public acknowledgement is expected.

Like the flame of a lamp, no follower of Jesus shines for their own sake.

While light may draw initial attention to itself, it never shines for its own sake. It shines to reveal something other than itself. You never hear a lit lamp state: "When am I ever going to get some credit around here? Don't they know that without me they will not be able to see?"

Those whose lives are conformed to the Beatitudes shine; their light illumines their good works as that which is for God's glory alone. They shun public applause. They are quick to deflect all praise to God alone. They confess the presence of good in or through them is because of Jesus alone.

As followers of Jesus we *are* light and we *do* shine.

Shining to invade the darkness of our world is our glorious burden.

Questions for reflection:

1. How does our culture express the idea of "light"?

2. How is that idea in line with or in contrast to the teaching of Jesus?

3. In what way does this teaching of Jesus challenge your own thinking?

4. Describe the value of you being light at home, work, school, and in public interactions.

12. DETAILS...

Jesus moves very quickly describing what His followers are to *be*: poor in spirit, broken, servants, hungry for righteousness, being mercy and peace, pure, and rejoicing because of persecution or opposition.

Enough material in a matter of minutes to occupy a lifetime.

He then informs us in what way such a life will invade the world: *salt* and *light.*

Simple words, but not an easy life. Simple truth, yet profound power. Simple assignment, but no easy task.

We are tempted to go into seclusion and focus of developing our "Beatitude being." We choose to believe that going into holy isolation is the only way to achieve and maintain such character.

Jesus never permits such a thing: "No. Go into the world. Penetrate the corruption and the darkness as salt and light."

Being what we so often are, we take such a life and such an assignment and pervert it into a never-ending series of lessons about salt and light. We talk about it among the uncorrupted in the light. And we just keep talking about it. We develop curriculum, study guides, leader's guides, and promo material. And we talk about it. We award certificates of completion to those who attended the classes and did the prescribed work. We know about salt and we know about light. Yet we are not being salt and light. We have yet to apply *being* to the very real issues of life. It is certainly easier to know than to be. It becomes easier to teach doing than to apply being.

This problem is not unique to the twenty-first century. It was present in the first century as well. Very likely present on that hill as Jesus gave the Sermon on the Mount.

I can see him sigh, then smile a patient smile, and continue.

He leaves no stone unturned!

13. THE LAW

Jesus has been speaking for a few moments without any mention of the law. The religious leaders and teachers did not, would not, speak without stating something from the law. These leaders and teachers developed quite a system of law: 248 laws stating things that must be done and 365 laws of prohibition for a total of 613 laws. It was enough to cause a sincere person to live on the edge of religious paranoia.

This teacher has presented challenging truth, painful even, but has done nothing to cause that level of paranoia. He has not mentioned anything about the Law. He seems more interested in being than in doing, more concerned about the power of presence than the bondage of systems.

Maybe he does not care about the law.

> **"Do not think I have come to abolish the Law or the Prophets; I have not come to abolish them but to fulfill them. I tell you the truth, until heaven and earth disappear, not the smallest letter, not the least stroke of a pen, will by any means disappear from the Law until everything is accomplished. Anyone who breaks one of the least of these commandments and teaches others to do the same**

will be called least in the kingdom of heaven, but whoever practices and teaches these commands will be called great in the kingdom of heaven. For I tell you that unless your righteousness surpasses that of the Pharisees and the teachers of the law, you will certainly not enter the kingdom of heaven." (vss. 17-20)

The Torah has been a central part of Israel's national life for centuries. The Torah is not viewed as simply the law: it is viewed as the revelation of God for His people. Faithful Jews taught the importance of keeping Torah. God has spoken. The proper response is to act in obedience. Obedience to Torah is tangible trust in the One True God. No faithful Jew believed the keeping of Torah creates righteousness; only God is the author of righteousness and obedience is in response to God's word and work.

The law was not given to create a legalistic system (a system that allowed someone to be defined as righteous by their own actions). The law was given to create a covenantal relationship.

By the time of first century this system of law has been perverted by a few religious leaders. It has been degraded from a covenantal relationship to a performance-based self-righteousness. A hint of this degrading can be seen in this story:

"Two men went up to the temple to pray, one a Pharisee and the other a tax collector. The Pharisee stood by himself and prayed: 'God, I thank you that I am not like other people – robbers, evildoers, adulterers – or even like this tax collector. I fast twice and week and give a tenth of all I get.'" (Luke 18:10-12)

This religious system allows someone to say, "I am righteous because I keep the law." It also allows someone to say, "You are a sinner because you do not keep the law."

That system is active among followers of Jesus in the twenty-first century as surely as it was in the first century.

There is something seductive about a performance-based system of legalism. This system allows me to create my own standard of righteousness by choosing a few select portions of Scripture (historical context, cultural context, and first audience considerations seldom have any impact on these selections). Most of these items are exclusively under my control: I can do or not do by making the choice and exercising a minimum of fleshly discipline. I am enabled to define myself as righteous, pointing to my own efforts as proof. This legalism is little more than the systems of the world dressed up in religious robes. This legalism is a false faith, an expression of selfish folly. This legalism is futile in the pursuit of true righteousness and covenantal relationship with the One True God.

Creating a check list of righteousness is much easier than to follow by faith. I find security, predictability, and affirmation in my check list. Week by week I am able to check the items and give myself the comfort of knowing I am righteous.

The things on my list are valuable; some are even necessary. The things on my list are not really the problem: the problem is that I allow that list to define righteousness on my terms.

Anytime that happens, be it in the first century or the twenty-first century, the intent of the law is perverted.

To introduce the law, God makes this declaration: **"I am the LORD your God, who brought you out of Egypt, ..."** **(Exodus 20:2)** Again and again, as the law is being given to Moses, God declares "I am the LORD your God." Again and again, He states, "I am the One who makes you Holy." The law is given to express a relational covenant: I am the LORD your God, the One Who makes you holy and you are my people. No other nation or people group has such a covenant, such a relational experience with any deity. No other nation or people group has such an expression of covenant as God's chosen people. Israel's God expects that every part of life express the relational covenant between Him and His people.

Take relationship out of the covenant and all that is left is law without redemption, performance without righteousness. All is frustration and futility as man attempts to appease some distant and demanding God.

When Jesus declares, **"I have not come to abolish the law"** he is not referring to the performance religion of that day; he is referring to the law in its original intent. He did not come to affirm religion: he came to establish the covenantal relationship.

His words help us understand that there are no unimportant parts in a covenantal relationship. The law, so understood, would not cease until all is accomplished. The law, so understood, requires our most careful attention, our most diligent discipline.

He also makes this startling statement: **"I have not come to abolish them** (the law) **but to *fulfill them."* *(emphasis added)*

The word translated 'fulfill' can just as easily and accurately be translated *complete.*

Jesus is the completion of the law.

I am only now coming to an elementary understanding of this. Please forgive my bumbling attempts to present what I believe will unfold as an astounding truth.

We have divided the law into three parts: ceremonial laws which govern the rituals of worship; civil law meant to govern daily life; and the moral law, most particularly the Ten Commandments.

We state the first category, ceremonial law, is no longer valid since the sacrificial death of Christ. We state the second category, the civil law, does not transfer in detail to our day, but does contain principles we should receive. We then affirm the third category, moral law – most particularly the Ten Commandments – is still in full force as much today as when it was originally given.

I believe we are mistaken.

The people of Israel did not receive the law as a trilogy. First century Jews would look at us in bewilderment as we explain to them the supposed three-fold nature of the law. The law was given and received as an undivided unit.

We are not to understand Jesus to say, "I have come to fulfill the sacrificial system, to transfer principled truths of the civil law, and to renew the strength of the Ten Commandments."

He said "I have come to bring the law to its completion."

All the law.

All the law, as an undivided unit, anticipates the coming of Christ. All the law, as an undivided unit, points to the coming Messiah. All the law, as an undivided unit, finds its ultimate expression in the person of Jesus.

Without Jesus, the law makes no sense. Without Jesus, the law becomes another system of religion. Without Jesus, the law is empty.

Jesus came to create a new and lasting covenant through his blood, a covenant whereby we may enter into lasting and righteous relationship with the Father.

We must not demand Jesus *and* civil law. We must not demand Jesus *and* the Ten Commandments.

To believe such is to miss the intention of the blood bought covenant: *relationship with the Father through the person of Jesus Christ alone.*

We are given a supernatural glimpse at a symbolic completion of the Law in the following account from **Luke 9:28-36 –**

> **"About eight days after Jesus said this, he took Peter, John and James with him and went up onto the mountain to pray. As he was praying, the appearance of his face changed, and his clothes became as bright as a flash of lightening. Two men, Moses and Elijah, appeared in glorious splendor, talking with Jesus. They spoke about his departure,**

which he was about to bring to fulfillment at Jerusalem. Peter and his companions were very sleepy, but when they became fully awake, they saw his glory and the two men standing with him. As the men were leaving Jesus, Peter said to him, 'Master, it is good for us to be here. Let us put up three shelters – one for you, one for Moses and one for Elijah.' (He did not know what he was saying.) While he was speaking, a cloud appeared and covered them, and they were afraid as they entered the cloud. A voice came from the cloud, saying, 'This is my son, whom I have chosen; listen to him.' When the voice had spoken, they found that Jesus was alone. The disciples kept this to themselves and did not tell anyone at the time what they had seen."

The glory of the law is depicted in Moses. The glory of the prophets is depicted by Elijah. The glory of the One who is the completion of both is seen in Christ. All in sacred conversation about what was soon to come: *the fulfillment at Jerusalem.* From the glorious cloud comes the Voice demanding the Son be heard. When the cloud lifts, the law and the prophets are gone – only Jesus remained.

Only Jesus.

All the law, all the prophets, find their ultimate completion in Jesus. The divine motive of the law and prophets – a relational covenant with the God of heaven

– is fully accomplished by the work of Christ upon the cross.

"See what great love the Father has lavished on us, that we should be called children of God!" (1 John 3:1)

Hallelujah!

This is the only way to make sense of the next statement of Jesus: **"For I tell you that unless your righteousness surpasses that of the Pharisees and the teachers of the law, you will certainly not enter the kingdom of heaven."**

Jesus is not saying that we must replace one system of law with another system of law. He is not saying that we need more law or greater law. He is not advocating a longer check list of righteousness.

The only surpassing righteousness is *Him*. He is saying that without the relational covenant with the Father that He, the completion of the law and prophets, provides we cannot be citizens of His Kingdom.

This sets the tone for the series of teachings that are about to be presented: **"You have heard it said…but I say…."**

Living by a system of performance is much easier than the journey Jesus insists we take.

This journey is not for the faint of heart. The journey is not for those who seek to avoid the exposure of their inmost life. The journey is not for those who prefer the comfort of hypocrisy in the shadow of their performance.

The journey ahead is only for those in whom the principles of the Beatitudes are fully at work. It is for those who will follow Jesus without regard to the cost. It is for those who will follow Jesus without complaint at the difficulty. It is for those who are more concerned about relationship with the Father through Jesus than about false dignity among men by keeping the law.

I enter the journey with fear and trembling.

Join me.

Questions for reflection:

1. What value does our culture place on performance?

2. In what ways does our culture judge someone by their appearance?

3. How has this mindset invaded the church?

4. How has this mindset affected your Christian experience?

5. What will it take to see and accept Jesus as enough?

14. ANGER

After declaring Himself as the completion of the law, Jesus begins to flesh out what that means for citizens in his Kingdom. With great authority, as One Who is fully capable to speak for and as the law, Jesus begins:

> "You have heard it said to the people long ago, 'Do not murder, and anyone who murders will be subject to judgment.' But I tell you that anyone who is angry with his brother will be subject to judgment. Again, anyone who says to his brother 'Raca' is answerable to the Sanhedrin. But anyone who says, 'You fool!' will be in danger of the fire of hell. Therefore, if you are offering your gift at the altar and there remember that your brother has something against you, leave your gift there in front of the altar. First go and be reconciled to your brother; then come and offer your gift. Settle matters quickly with your adversary who is taking you to court. Do it while you are still with him on the way, or he may hand you over to the judge, and the judge may hand you over to the officer, and you may be thrown into prison. I tell you the truth, you will not get out until you have paid the last penny."
> (vss. 21-26)

Most, if not all, the listeners on the mountain that day could declare, "I have not murdered anyone, so I have kept the law." They could quickly and honestly check that box.

I believe that most of those reading these words today could testify to the same measure of obedience: "I have not murdered anyone." We, too, could quickly and honestly check that box.

And once again we exercise a particular skill when it comes to the teachings of Jesus: *missing the point.*

Jesus is not presenting a check list. He is mandating that we engage in a heart check. He is leading us down an uncomfortable path toward the issues of the heart.

Consider this paraphrase of the words of Jesus: "I am not giving you a list of behavior boxes to check through discipline. I am leading you to the spirit of the law as expressed by this command: love one another as I have loved you."

He begins this journey, not with the issue of murder, but with the issue of anger.

I have heard, and likely have said, "Sin is sin is sin. God sees all sin the same." Even though we say such a thing we are inconsistent in its application, indicating by our practice we don't really believe what we say. We excuse certain lesser sins and accuse those more horrifying sins.

We give gossip a free pass, offering no disciplinary action. If someone embezzles church funds that is a different matter. We lie to our kids (little white lies of course) but call for the firing of a coach who yells at our child. We mean well but I believe we are a bit misinformed, or at the very least our words offer incorrect implications.

Nowhere in the Scriptures do we find all sins being treated as equally evil. Some sins are prescribed the punishment of death. Some sins are prescribed the punishment of restitution and restoration. John writes some challenging words that mark a difference between sins that lead to death and sins that do not lead to death (see **1 John 5**). Peter tells us that love covers a multitude of sins, clearly indicating some sins are not so evil as others (see **1 Peter 4**).

The Scriptures are consistent in declaring all sins as equally *guilty*. That is a different matter entirely.

We are mistaken if we hear Jesus say that murder and anger are equally evil. He is saying murder and being angry with a brother are equally guilty. Both are expressions of selfishness that are in contrast with the law of love. Both are in violation of what He declares as the greatest commandments which completely summed up all the law and prophets: an unreserved love for God and a love for others (see **Mark 12:31-32**).

Those on that mountain could have responded, "Got it. I should not harbor a murderous rage toward my brother." We would immediately nod in agreement and believe we have grasped this truth. Check the box!

They, and we, would be right. Right, but incomplete. Jesus does what He always does: invites us to follow Him further along the journey toward being complete, not just being right.

He expands this truth by saying if we give expression to our anger by using degrading language toward another person we are guilty.

Let me see if I can quote where our minds are going about now: "Got it. I have never, and will never, say 'Raca' to anyone. I will always be careful to never call anyone a 'fool' from now on."

Throughout my Christian journey I have repeatedly heard someone declare, "Jesus said if we call someone a fool we are in danger of going to hell!" We learned the spiritual art of gasping in horror if we ever heard someone call anyone a fool, even if it was in jest.

And once again we exercise one of our greatest gifts: *missing the point.* That is what we do when we take the teachings of Jesus and create a check list out of what was intended as a heart check.

Let's be honest enough to admit: most of us have default words or phrases we use when we are angry with someone. Terms that are meant to degrade, belittle, demean or injure the person with whom we are angry. The particular words are not the issue: the motive of the heart is the issue.

Consider these strong words from John: **"Anyone who hates another brother or sister is really a murderer at heart. And you know that murderers don't have eternal life within them"** (**1 John 3:15** NLT). Words meant to injure or degrade are birthed by hatred: if we are not loving the person, if we are not working for their good, if the attitude we express is angry and hurtful, those words and attitudes can only be defined as an expression of hate. John affirms the teaching of Jesus: murder and relational anger are equally guilty.

"Wait just a minute pastor. I don't hate anybody and I certainly have not and will not murder anybody. I don't appreciate you trying to make me feel guilty."

Let's take a short journey. Examine the following examples of relational anger that express hatred, even if temporary, to see if and where we might be guilty -

Parents to children: "You're so stupid!" "Can't you do anything right?" "You'll never amount to anything!" "Get out of my sight!"

Spouse to spouse: "All I ask is that you do _____; but noooo! I guess I just ask too much." "Really?! Wow!"

Person to person: "How stupid can you be? Think, think, think! Whew." "You idiot!"

To the waitress: "This food is awful. Do you really expect me to eat this? I can't believe you served me this junk. No tip for you!"

To the boss: "You can have this stupid job!"

To the pastor: "I am not getting fed. Sometimes I wonder if you even have a call to preach. I think you should just pack your bags and leave us alone."

The list is endless: painful, degrading and demeaning. *And guilty.*

There is another subtle form by which anger is expressed. This is found among those who never lose their temper, but wag their tongue. Those who never confront with firm grace, but converse in private whispers. Those who never think to ask, but are quick to assume. Those who do not talk with someone, but won't hesitate to talk about someone.

These passive/aggressive conversations are never meant to build up the absent person's reputation. They never shine a light on the good aspects or good deeds of the individual not included in the discussion. The end result of such conversations is never increased loyalty and relationship.

Most, if not all, conversations *about* someone rather than a conversation *with* that someone are meant to tear down, degrade, belittle, hinder, damage, force out. As such, it is condemned by this teaching of Jesus.

Here are a few questions to ask about our conversations:

Would I say this directly to the person? If the answer is "yes", then do just that. If the offered answer is "yes" and we still engage in conversation about them in their absence, we are involved in gossip, we are guilty and we live in a delusion.

What would be my reaction if the absent person about whom I am talking suddenly sat down next to me? If embarrassment and an awkward change in the conversation would be our reaction, we are probably involved in gossip and are guilty.

What effect is this conversation having on the absent person's reputation? If the answer is anything other than edifying then we are involved in gossip and are guilty.

Gossip and murder are not equally evil but they are equally guilty.

The dynamics have changed dramatically, both on that mountain and in the room where we are sitting. How many of them, how many of us, can testify that we have never (and are not now) angry with someone? How many of them, how many of us, can testify that we have not spoken to or about someone in a degrading way?

That is what I thought: we are all guilty.

Jesus then takes us yet another step into the reality of the issue. He informs us that if no attempt has been made to reconcile the issue of our anger with another person *then our guilt remains and our worship is in vain.*

Jesus changes the tone of the issue at this point. If I am tracking with Him correctly this is what I hear:

> "If you make no attempt to be reconciled with the brother you injured with your anger, then know this: your worship is in vain and that brother will become your adversary. I will not interfere with what happens next. Whatever happens to you as a result of your unresolved relational anger is the reaping of what you've sown. You best move quickly to resolve this."

We need to understand: unresolved relational anger carries an inevitable and unavoidable cost.

We have seen it over and over. A broken friendship. A ruined marriage. A church split. A pastor who leaves the ministry. A church member who forsakes the church. Children who will not speak to their parents. Parents who have disowned their children. Neighbors who no longer speak.

All these can check the box *Do not murder*. But none can declare they are guiltless.

There is only one process for a citizen in Christ's Kingdom to deal with such relational anger:

We must recognize such anger is a violation of the law of love and as such makes us transgressors.

We must accept the guilt for such transgression.

We must confess the anger for what it is: *sin.*

We must make an attempt at reconciliation before engaging in the next act of worship.

I think if we offered immediate and literal obedience on this issue two things would happen: a church service would experience tremendous disruption as people leave or step across the aisle to make an attempt at reconciliation; and an incredible spiritual renewal would begin as Christ's Kingdom breaks in.

Can you imagine such a moment? Can you picture this Divine disruption in our carefully crafted service plans? Anger and gossip being confessed. Grudges being cleansed. Restitutions being made. Tearful embraces as forgiveness flows in all directions. What a moment of rebirth for individuals and the church. What a moment of Holy Spirit re-creation as people are made new through the grace of Christ. The transformation would be profound.

"Lord, make it so in me! Make it so in those who are reading this. Make it so in our churches. Make it so in our family relationships. Make it so at work and at school."

Questions for reflection:

1. How does our culture look at the issue of relational anger?

2. How has this perspective on relational anger influenced the church?

3. In what way(s) have you expressed relational anger? What impact did that have on the relationship(s)?

4. Are you angry with someone right now? Are you holding a grudge against someone right now? Have you talked about that person rather than to that person?

5. In light of this teaching of Jesus, what should you do before the next worship event in your life?

15. LUST

What a journey. Jesus has been leading the crowd on that mountain, and leading us, deeply into His Kingdom. He is clarifying that the kingdom of this world and His Kingdom are in contrast and cannot be reconciled. Those who are citizens of His Kingdom, those who submit to His authority, are required to live to a different standard, to embrace higher values.

Not simply different or higher: the standard of His Kingdom is *holiness*.

This holiness is not found in, nor expressed by, righteousness check lists, no matter how badly we wish it were so.

This holiness is not found through stringent discipline. Such holiness would simply be self-righteousness attainable to anyone willing to exercise such discipline.

This holiness is only found by submitting to the King of the Kingdom, the only One who is able and authorized to cause holiness to be a working reality in and through the citizens of His Kingdom.

This demand of holiness digs deeply today:

"You have heard that it was said, 'Do not commit adultery.' But I tell you that anyone who looks at a woman lustfully has already committed adultery with her in his heart. If your right eye causes you to sin, gouge it out and throw it away. It is better for you to lose one part of your body than for your whole body to be thrown into hell. And if you right hand causes you to sin, cut it off and throw it away. It is better for you to lose one part of your body than for your whole body to go to hell." (vss. 27-30)

The desire for sexual intimacy is within us by the design of our Creator God. He pronounced that desire, along with all the other aspects of His creative work, "very good" (see **Genesis 1:31**). In His eternal wisdom he placed boundaries along the path of sexual discovery and fulfillment. For all who will live and practice within those boundaries, sexual intimacy is good, healthy, and holy.

The journey of sexual discovery always has a moment. That moment was aptly described by some teenage boys in the church I pastor. I asked if they were excited about going into high school. They gave a quick response, "Yes!" When asked why such excitement they replied, "Cause girls ain't guys no more." I grinned and said, "Ah, you've noticed, have you?" It is good, healthy, even holy, that these boys noticed that exciting difference. I am hopeful that I and this church can influence these boys to make good decisions as they take this journey of discovery.

Our culture certainly is not helping them. Sexuality is shown as instinctual, animalistic, uncontrollable, even a right. Adolescents are being influenced toward hypersexual choices in clothing and behavior. My spirit weeps when I see young girls dressing and behaving in ways that send a message of sensuality. I am saddened when I see young boys acting out sexualized behavior and having sexualized conversations. This becomes fertile soil in which lust will grow out of control.

Our hypersexualized culture is destroying any hope of sexual intimacy being good, healthy, and holy. It is mutating sexual intimacy into nothing more than the cruel urges of uncontrollable lust.

> "Our culture seems to teach us that mind-blowing sex for a lifetime is the 'Holy Grail' we all should seek. If we watch any TV, listen to any popular music, look at any magazine rack, or see any movies, we will be tempted to think that the whole world is either having sex or figuring out ways to have it better." [13]

Girls (and women) are flaunting and guys (and men) are leering. And love is losing its meaning.

---

[13] Ralph Earle and Mark Lasser, *The Pornography Trap,* (Kansas City, MO: Beacon Hill Press of Kansas City, 2002), pgs. 45-46.

Lust cannot form a foundation upon which a lifetime of intimacy can be built. When the fire of lust burns dim, a new object will be sought to excite that fire again.

"Jerry worked with me at the Alamo Plaza Motel in Nashville. We were both working our way through college. I remember the night he came into the office and slumped on the couch. I was working on the night transcript, and he began muttering to himself, meaning to be overheard by me. 'I don't get it. Here you are a virgin, dating a great girl, never had sex and don't intend to until you're married. I've had more women than I can remember. You feel loved and valued. I'm miserable and lonely. I don't get it.' It must have been divine inspiration that hit me in the middle of the night. 'Jerry, I do get it. You are destroying your capacity to love. Every night, you practice bonding and breaking, bonding and breaking. Sexual intercourse binds two people in a covenant of marriage for life. It is a bonding act. When you bind yourself to a person that you hardly know and walk out of the room never intending to see that person again, you damage your capacity to love. You are learning to love and leave, not love and stay. It doesn't surprise me that you feel lonely. You've been doing nothing but using your fellow humans and treating women like conquests in a game. My goal for sex is to love and stay, bind myself in marriage to one person and stay bound for the rest of my life. Call it boring. Call it conservative. I call it love as God intended it to be.' I don't know if my motel sermon moved him or not. But I still believe what I said that night." [14]

In order for the pursuit of sexual intimacy to be appropriate, blessed, and satisfying it must be built upon an unreserved love for God.

These principles are true now and they were true on the mountain that day so long ago.

Those first century listeners knew nothing of a pornographic industry – no VHS, no DVD, no adult film industry. No push button access through pay-per-view or the web. No discreetly wrapped magazine delivered to a post office box.

It would be naïve of us to believe those first century listeners lived with less sexual tension, less sexual temptation, less interest in the discovery of sexual intimacy. All we need do is go back and read Old Testament history. The Bible makes no effort to hide the ugliness of sexual sin and its consequences. The Bible

---

[14] Dan Boone, *Charitable Discourse: talking about the things that divide us,* (Kansas City, MO: Beacon Hill Press of Kansas City, 2010), pg. 77.

speaks without blushing of sexual intimacy in the **Song of Solomon** (please, do not read this beautiful story as only an allegory of the relationship between God and Israel or Christ and the Church!).

Sexual lust has always been an ugly consuming monster.

Lust, the desire to have, to consume, to indulge without restraint and without regard for the consequences. *Lust,* this ultimate expression of selfishness. *Lust*, that demands satisfaction no matter the cost, no matter the destruction, no matter the pain.

Lust, by which Satan perverts the beauty of God's gracious and good gift of human sexuality.

Today lust is big business. According to abc.go.com and nbc.news.com the porn industry in America generates more money than the National Football League, the National Basketball Association and Major League Baseball *combined.* Revenue in the US is $10 -$12 billion a year. Globally, the porn industry generates nearly $100 billion a year.

Sabrina, founder and director of *New Creation VA* – a non-profit organization that combats human trafficking - stated in a ministerial meeting I attended in February of 2017: "Pornography is human trafficking" (for more information about *New Creation VA* and the issue of human trafficking visit www.newcreationVA.org). We are surrounded by sensual imagery: magazine covers, store window displays, movies, TV, sporting events, and just walking down the street. Images meant to incite lust are available with the touch of a screen. Our young ladies are being sold a false image and being demanded to meet an impossible standard. Our young men are being sold a fantasy. It all sets a standard of beauty and sexiness that is both unrealistic and unsustainable. This makes our young men and women vulnerable to sexual predators interested only in human trafficking.

The invitation to lust is everywhere.

I remember the day, at about 10 or 11 years old, when I found a soft porn magazine near my favorite fishing hole. It scared me to death. A woman's body will do that to a boy...and to a man. That body is frightening, mysterious, beautiful, alluring, unforgettable. It has been the inspiration for music, art, poetry, movies, even war. It has been the subject of explicit expression in the Bible: ever read the **Song of Solomon**? This body is designed by the Creator God. It is meant to be respected, admired, enjoyed and protected. It is not meant to be exploited or carelessly exposed. Christians should understand this better than anybody. Christian men should be examples of righteous morality when it comes to a woman's body. Christian women should be examples of righteous modesty when it comes to their own body. A woman's body is too precious, too glorious, to be treated any other way.

Lust is and always has been bad business. It creates merciless addiction. According to www.addictionhope.com twelve million people in the US are captured by an addiction to pornography. Lust destroys integrity in a moment. It ruins relationships. It victimizes the vulnerable. It abuses the innocent. It offers fantasy but delivers fire. Lust is an unrelenting monster.

Lust alters the ability of the brain to process logical thought. The brain communicates within itself by way of neurons. These neurons travel through the brain by way of neural pathways. When the thought patterns of the brain are repetitively focused on a particular subject, that pathway becomes engrained in the brain by that repetition. Other neural pathways wither through neglect. If an individual observes lustful images again and again, a new neural pathway is formed. This neural pathway has the power to give the brain a new default mode which creates an addiction. Listen to this horrifying story told by a woman about her husband:

> "After indulging in fantasy for more than 20 years,
> Jack lost his ability to think about anything else.
> Dwelling so much on that which wasn't true made
> him unable to think about that which was true. He
> lost his common sense and his ability to solve
> problems. My husband, once a brilliant engineer,
> couldn't even figure out how to turn a freezer so it
> would fit through the door into the cellar. He was

absentminded to the extreme. Sometimes, when someone would ask him a question, he would start to answer, only to stop halfway into the reply and then freeze with his mouth open. His mind had gone completely blank. Too much time fantasizing meant he also lost his ability to do his work well. Finally, the man who was recognized three times as an outstanding employee was fired for being incompetent and lying to his boss. Once a regional manager for a large company...today he is doing production work, packing 12-ounce bags of chocolates at $7.25 an hour. Jack had blown his mind on fantasy." [15]

According the Jesus, lust is always *guilty.*

Lust is a sexual sin that is equally guilty with committing adultery.

Conquering lust requires a strong, sacrificial, and sanctified response.

Jesus worded it in a strange way: **"...gouge out your eye...cut off your hand...."**

He knew, and we know, that an eye could be gouged out and a hand be cut off and lust still be an active and consuming monster. He is making a point in a way those

---

[15] Laurie Hall, *An Affair of the Mind,* (Colorado Springs, CO: Focus on the Family Publishing, 1996), pgs. 98-99.

listeners would understand, and that we must understand: *take strong, sacrificial action against lust.*

The loss of an eye indicates the loss of sight. Could it be that Jesus is mandating that we change how we see, how we perceive?

Early each calendar year, *Sports Illustrated* produces its swimsuit edition. The cover model is beautiful and alluring, inviting us to turn the pages and indulge our lustful desires.

I believe Jesus would have us change our response when we see this edition on display. Rather than turning a blinded eye, maybe he is asking that we change our perspective. Rather than an object of lust, maybe that young lady should be a reminder of the thousands of young ladies who are lost, confused, abused, crying out for attention, believing that their body is the only tool they have to be noticed, to be loved. Rather than turning away in disgust, maybe Jesus would have us breathe a prayer. Maybe He would have us go to someone trapped in the delusions of sinful sexuality and give them hope as it is in Him.

"Lord, help us to see others as You see them!"

The loss of a hand indicates a dramatic loss of activity. We all know those areas, those channels, those web searches that create an opportunity for lust. Jesus would have us dramatically change our activity patterns. Stop the surfing. Stop the carnal curiosity. Avoid those areas that have drawn you into lustful thinking. Avoid those times and places that have proven to be times and places of temptation. After speaking so powerfully of those who lived and died by faith, the Apostle Paul said this: **"Therefore, since we are surrounded by such a great cloud of witnesses, let us throw off everything that hinders and the sin that so easily entangles, and let us run with perseverance the race marked out for us."** **(Hebrews 12:1)**

Avoid the invitation to lust as surely as you would avoid an invitation to commit adultery.

It could be that on the other side of the issue, we are being asked to stop presenting ourselves as invitations to lust.

After preaching a message on modesty, a teenage girl expressed interest in better understanding that issue. I had watched her grow from a cute little girl into an awkward 'tweener' and now into a beautiful teenage young lady. I acknowledged that she had grown into a beautiful young lady and having a desire to be attractive was entirely appropriate. Then I gave her two illustrations: one morning she dresses for school in a way that flatters her attractiveness. As she walks down the hall of her high school a boy sees her and thinks "Wow, she's beautiful!" The next day she dresses in a way that flaunts her developing body. As she walks down the hall

142

of her high school a boy sees her and thinks "I've got to get me some of that!" The first is modest, the other is not. She looked at me, smiled, and said "I get it."

Please, don't misunderstand me. Women are not the only ones at fault. Yes, they often present themselves, even in church, in ways that invite lust. Those women are answerable to God for how they present themselves, both in their dress and in their manner. And we, the men, are fully accountable to the same God for how we chose to respond to what is sometimes forced into our line of sight.

Jesus says to both of us, the men and the women: make a dramatic change and stop being a participant in the sinful cycle of lust.

Once again Jesus removes the satisfaction of a check list and replaces it with the much more demanding heart-check.

From religion to holiness.

We must choose.

Only through the sanctifying grace of God through Christ that human sexuality can be what God intends it to be: pure, holy, and pleasing to God and to us. Battling lust any other way will soon cause us to view sexuality as dirty, dangerous, and shameful.

I am determined, and invite you to join me, to keep my sexuality under the sanctifying grace of God through Christ. Only then will we see it as the beautiful thing it is meant to be. Only then will we express it within the boundaries God has clearly established.

This will enable us to live in the beauty of our design and in the restful place of holiness.

Questions for reflection:

1. Give some examples of how our culture views human sexuality.

2. How has this cultural view of human sexuality influenced the church?

3. Describe your 'journey of discovery.'

5. In what ways do you give expression to your own desire for sexual expression?

6. How do these expression line up with the teachings of Jesus?

7. What guards are in place in your life to protect your sexual integrity?

16. DIVORCE AND REMARRIAGE

As a boy growing up in the conservative element of the church world, nothing caused more heated discussion than the issue of divorce and remarriage. Most of these youthful discussions were governed more by heat than by light. Listening to pastors and evangelists did not help. Some preached hell and damnation, others preached love and indulgence and still others avoided the issue completely. I was never involved in, nor have I ever observed, a charitable discussion on the issue. I did see the issue separate friends, split churches and even divide denominations.

Divorce and remarriage has always been a difficult and dangerous issue to address.

Jesus addresses divorce and remarriage next.

There are two broad dangers in dealing with the issue:

The danger of pride is a reality for those whose lives are unaffected by divorce/remarriage. From this position of pride these individuals often look down upon those who are divorced and remarried. Words and attitudes express condemnation, denial of fellowship and unreasonable demands. An atmosphere of "us" versus "them" results with no regard for pain or for grace.

Those whose life is affected by divorce and remarriage are often easily offended when they perceive any challenge on the issue. From that offense they become defensive and angry. Many act as though there should only be understanding with never any negative consequences for either the divorce or the remarriage. They often interpret Scripture by their experience rather than defining their experience by Scripture.

All of us can find it difficult to submit to the authority of Scripture on this issue.

I prayerfully trust no one reading this chapter will fall victim to either of these dangers. Let us remember that God's grace is enough to conquer our unwarranted pride and temper our temper.

So, breathe deep and let's take a look.

> **"It has been said, 'Anyone who divorces his wife must give her a certificate of divorce.' But I tell you that anyone who divorces his wife, except for marital unfaithfulness, causes her to become an adulteress, and anyone who marries the divorced woman commits adultery."** (vss. 31-32)

In order to gain a fuller understanding, it is important we examine the words of Jesus on this issue in other contexts:

"Some Pharisees came to him to test him. They asked, 'Is it lawful for a man to divorce his wife for any and every reason?' 'Haven't you read,' he replied, 'that at the beginning the Creator 'made them male and female,' and said, 'for this reason a man will leave his father and mother and be united to his wife, and the two will become one flesh'? So they are no longer two, but one. Therefore what God has joined together, let man not separate.' 'Why then,' they asked, 'did Moses command that a man give his wife a certificate of divorce and send her away?' Jesus replied, 'Moses permitted you to divorce your wives because your hearts were hard. But it was not this way from the beginning. I tell you that anyone who divorces his wife, except for marital unfaithfulness, and marries another woman commits adultery.'" (Matthew 19:3-9; Mark 10:2-12 is almost an identical account; **Mark** does include a woman as the one initiating the divorce.)

"Anyone who divorces his wife and marries another woman commits adultery, and the man who marries a divorced woman commits adultery." (Luke 16:18)

The Apostle Paul address this issue:

"Do you not know, brothers – for I am speaking to men who know the law – that the law has authority over a man only as long as he lives? For example, by law a married woman is bound to her husband as long as he is alive, but if her husband dies, she is released from the law of marriage. So then, if she marries another man while her husband is alive, she is called an adulteress. But if her husband dies, she is released from that law and is not an adulteress, even though she marries another man." (Romans 7:1-3)

"To the married I give this command (not I, but the Lord): a wife must not separate from her husband. But if she does, she must remain unmarried or else be reconciled to her husband. And a husband must not divorce his wife." (1 Corinthians 7:10-11)

"A woman is bound to her husband as long as he lives. But if her husband dies, she is free to marry anyone she wishes, but he must belong to the Lord." (1 Corinthians 7:39)

When approaching the subject of marriage, divorce and remarriage we must go back to the beginning.

The sacredness of marriage is found in the Divine design of the first man: **"Then God said, 'Let us make man in our image and likeness.' So God created man in his image." (Genesis 1:26,27)**

Original man was purposefully designed to bear the image and likeness of God. There exists something mysterious, wonderful and fearful about the design of original man (could the Psalmist be expressing some insight into this truth in **Psalm 139:14**?). At some undetermined later time, God performed a surgery of separation, taking woman out of man (**Genesis 2:18-23**). The image and likeness of God are now incompletely displayed by two distinct and unique individuals.

It is at this point that God institutes heterosexual marriage: **"So a man will leave his father and mother and be united with his wife, and the two will become one body." (Genesis 2:24**). Through the sacred covenant of marriage, God not only provided for procreation and pleasure, He also made possible for the mystery of His image and likeness to be more perfectly and fully displayed. Through the marriage covenant, a man and woman are symbolically returned to the original design of man – united as one in imitation of the loving fellowship and unity of the Trinity.

When tested by the Pharisees in **Matthew 19 (Mark 10)** Jesus points back to this creation/recreation event. He then clearly declares marriage, both its union and its dissolution, as God's domain: **"What God has joined together, let no man separate."**

Nowhere in the teachings of Scripture on marriage does God mandate the issue of divorce. Jesus declares that divorce is a legal concession provided by Moses because of the sinfulness of the human heart. Divorce is a sinful intrusion into the original plan of the Creator.

It is unimaginable that a husband and wife, who are following Jesus, loving God without reserve and loving others, bearing the image of God and the fruit of the Spirit, would *ever* give cause for the issue of divorce to arise. They understand that the opposite of divorce is not marriage: the opposite of divorce is *holiness*.

We live in a fallen world and when sin is allowed to live in our hearts the potential for divorce is conceived. Jesus indicates that the one possible allowance for divorce is the sin of sexual unfaithfulness to the marriage covenant. He does not demand divorce in such cases and divorce does not suddenly find its place in God's plan as the result of such devastating sin.

Yes – *devastating*. Not a mistake. Not just a tryst. Not just a moment of weakness. Sexual unfaithfulness to the marriage covenant is devastating.

Try this: take two pieces of paper. Write your name on one piece and the name of your spouse on the other. Now glue to two sheets together, names facing one another. After a week get those united pieces and separate them. The result: devastation to both pieces.

I used this example in premarital counseling not long ago. I was able to observe the physical impact of this lesson as that precious couple worked to separate those sheets of paper. Silence settled on the office as we all just sat there a moment. Finally, a very quiet, "Wow."

Jesus taught us that it is Satan's business to steal, kill, and destroy.

Sexual unfaithfulness to the marriage covenant is one of his great tools that often accomplishes all three with overwhelming force.

Live in holiness! It is the only sufficient safeguard for marriage.

If I understand the teachings of Jesus on this issue, divorce without sexual unfaithfulness as its cause does not dissolve the marriage.

Any remarriage after a non-allowable divorce is declared as adultery: the dissolution of the previous marriage is not recognized.

In this teaching of Jesus, permission to remarry is not implicit in the possible allowance for divorce. It might be implied but it is not clearly expressed. Even if implied, it would be for the non-offending spouse only. It is unthinkable that the God of marriage would grant permission to remarry to the unfaithful spouse as the result of desecrating His plan through an act of gross immorality. The reward for the sinful dissolution of the first marriage is the 'blessing' of a second marriage? In a culture that is narcissistic to the core the answer to that unimaginable question is "yes!"

The only clearly expressed permission for remarriage is after one of the marital partners dies (see **Romans 7** and **1 Cor. 7**).

In all of this a great truth arises: marriage is more, so much more, than just a piece of paper granted by the courthouse and signed by the officiating clergy.

God is the Originator and Creator of marriage. It is a high and holy covenant and cannot be dissolved easily. Just as a piece of paper from the courthouse cannot create marriage, neither can a piece of paper from the courthouse dissolve a marriage.

Marriage is God's domain. He made marriage and He dissolves marriage through the death of a spouse.

What are we to do with this hard truth?

We must learn to acknowledge the sacredness of the marital covenant, live under the authority of that covenant, and insist upon its authority in our living, teaching, preaching and church government. In so doing we must model Christ, Who was full of grace and truth. We must stand upon the truth of the Word, but never with a stance that is devoid of grace.

We must learn to acknowledge that divorce is not a part of God's plan: it is clearly a sinful intrusion. Always live, teach, preach and counsel away from divorce toward the authority of marital covenant and the Author of the covenant, Who is able to restore all things.

We must learn to acknowledge that grace is enough to sustain a life-long marriage. Grace will not make it glamorous, 'hot', pain free, or without difficulty. Grace will make it possible. Not only possible but incredibly rewarding.

We must learn to acknowledge that grace is enough for those who have been divorced – even if that means, as it may, that they remain single for the rest of their life.

We must learn to acknowledge that grace is enough for those who have remarried contrary to Scripture. God's grace through Christ will grant forgiveness and enable the present marriage to be lived with integrity and faithfulness as that marriage is brought under the authority of the truth of the Word.

Before we leave this issue, let us remember the woman at the well (**John 4**). Jesus knew her sinful history of divorce and remarriage, and her current sinful condition. Yet he did not offer her condemnation: He offered her Living Water which would make her an heir of eternal life.

We all need grace: the forgiving and cleansing grace of God through Christ and the gift of grace granted to one another.

154

~~~~

Is there any question that the Kingdom of Christ is a Kingdom in stark contrast to the kingdoms of this world?

Questions for reflection:

1. How does our culture view the issue of divorce?

2. How has this view changed the issue of marriage in our culture?

3. How has the cultural perspective on divorce and remarriage impacted the church?

4. How has your family, immediate or extended, been impacted by divorce?

5. How does the 'grace and truth' of this teaching of Jesus need to touch your life? How can you take this 'grace and truth' and touch the life of someone else?

17. OATHS

We live in a culture of suspicion and dishonesty.

We assume politicians are lying. We are quick to suspect that the mechanic is not being completely honest about the need or the cost of repairs. We are taught to consider every anonymous phone call a scam. When eating out we are hesitant to complain about our steak: the cook may spit on it if we send it back. We have lost the ability to be surprised when we hear about a corrupt police officer, mayor, or local pastor.

We have learned by experience and observation to mistrust others until such mistrust is proven unfounded.

I remember hearing a mother tell her teen son, who was an admitted liar, she had lied to him without him even knowing. I guess she was trying to convince him that she, his mother, was a better liar.

Several years ago, I was contracted to build a large deck around an above ground swimming pool. After digging the post holes for the anchor portion of that deck I called for an inspection. The inspector passed those holes without challenge. "I have about 50 more post holes to dig. They will all be just like these. Could you just wave me through? I will call you for the framing inspection."

His reply: "So you say. Call me when you get more holes dug."

Ugh.

We must sign *everything* from the swipe screen at the local hardware for $6.87 to mountains of mortgage papers. Everybody, businesses and individuals alike, must exercise constant vigilance against those who are dishonest.

Have you ever had an occasion when someone asked for something and promised to bring it back, to repay the loan, or repay the favor with these words: "I swear on a stack of Bibles...on my mother's grave...."?

When someone offers such a dramatic oath in an effort to convince me of their trustworthiness my immediate response is to disbelieve them.

But I jump ahead.

Consider the words of Jesus:

> **"Again, you have heard that it was said to the people long ago, 'Do not break your oath, but keep the oaths you have made to the Lord.' But I tell you, Do not swear at all: either by heaven, for it is God's throne; or by the earth, for it is his footstool; or by Jerusalem, for it is the city of the Great King. And do not swear by your head, for you cannot**

make even on hair white or black. Simply let your
'Yes' be 'Yes' and your 'No' 'No'; anything beyond
this comes from the evil one." (vss. 33-37)

While Old Testament law allowed for making an oath, it
also made it clear that an oath was binding, with only
two exceptions. A father could cancel the oath of a
daughter:

> "When a young woman still living in her father's
> household makes a vow to the LORD or obligates
> herself by a pledge, and her father hears about her
> vow or pledge but says nothing to her, then all her
> vows and every pledge by which she obligated
> herself will stand. But if her father forbids her
> when he hears about it, none of her vows or the
> pledges by which she obligated herself will stand;
> the LORD will release her because her father has
> forbidden her" (Numbers 30:3-5). A husband could
> cancel the oath of his wife: "Her husband may
> confirm or nullify any vow she makes or any sworn
> pledge to deny herself." (Numbers 30:13).   Many
> oaths contained a self-curse: "Then they all came
> and urged David to eat something while it was still
> day; but David took an oath, saying, 'May God deal
> with me, be it ever so severely, if I taste bread or
> anything else before the sun sets!'" (2 Samuel 3:35).

"An oath carries with it an explicit or implicit curse, if
the oath taken proves false or is violated. The phrase

'God do so and more also,' and introductory formula of an oath, is a distinct allusion to a self-imposed curse. Because making an oath is an act of holiness, its violation is a profanation of the name of God and subjects one to divine punishment."[16]

Those on the mountain that day were taught about making an oath from Old Testament law and were permitted to take an oath in the name of God. Failure to keep such a sworn oath profaned the name of God (see **Exodus 20:7** and **Leviticus 19:12**) and put them at serious risk of Divine judgment. **Deuteronomy 23:21-23** offers this clear explanation concerning an oath:

> **"If you make a vow to the LORD your God, do not be slow to pay it, for the LORD your God will certainly demand it of you and you will be guilty of sin. But if you refrain from making a vow, you will not be guilty. Whatever your lips utter you must be sure to do, because you made your vow freely to the LORD your God with you own mouth."**

Ecclesiastes offers these words of caution:

---

[16] Geoffrey Wigoder, General Editor, *Illustrated Dictionary and Concordance of the Bible,* (Jerusalem: The Jerusalem Publishing House LTD, 1986), pg. 742.

"When you make a vow to God, do not delay in fulfilling it. He has no pleasure in fools; fulfill your vow. It is better not to vow than to make a vow and not fulfill it. Do not let your mouth lead you into sin. And do not protest to the temple messenger, 'My vow was a mistake.' Why should God be angry at what you say and destroy the work of your hands?" (5:4-6)

The action promised on oath must be performed and the timing of that oath must be observed. The mouth bound the life until such time as the oath was performed.

The centuries between the Law and the time of Christ saw some perversions of the law of oaths. Jesus calls the leaders into account on this matter:

"Woe, to you, blind guides! You say, 'If anyone swears by the temple, it means nothing; but if anyone swears by the gold of the temple, his is bound by his oath.' You blind fools! Which is greater: the gold or the temple that makes the gold sacred? You also say, 'If anyone swears by the altar, it means nothing: but if anyone swears by the gift on it, he is bound by his oath.' You blind men! Which is greater: the gift, or the altar that makes the gift sacred? Therefore he who swears by the altar swears by it and by everything on it. And he who swears by the temple swears by it and by the one who dwells in it. And he who swears by heaven swears by God's throne and by the one who sits on it." (Matthew 23:16-22)

The religious leaders did what human nature drives us all to do: create exclusions and exceptions where none should exist. And Jesus responds to them like He does to us – He brings us to the heart of the matter where there are no loopholes.

Jesus' response to the issue of oath making was unequivocal: *"Do not swear at all."*

He then forbids the use of the binding agents that were most common in that day and culture: heaven, the earth, and the city of Jerusalem. Each of these has a connection to the very person of God: by invoking them you bring the name and person of God into the oath (as with the temple and the altar in **Matthew 23:16-22**). This was not to be done. Any oath made with our own head as the binding agent was useless: we have no power to change anything about ourselves, not even hair color, by concentration of thought.

This teaching of Christ is a radical departure from the cultural practices of the kingdoms of the world. Oath making in its various forms was a common, maybe even expected, practice in personal and business interactions.

Jesus once again clarifies the contrast between the kingdoms of the world and His Kingdom when he declares "**do not swear at all.**"

We must also recognize the futility of making oaths, or even promises, which require the future becoming a present reality. James addresses this futility:

> **"Now listen, you who say, 'Today or tomorrow we will go to this or that city, spend a year there, carry on business and make money.' Why, you do not even know what will happen tomorrow. What is your life? You are a mist that appears for a little while and then vanishes. Instead, you ought to say, 'If it is the Lord's will, we will live and do this or that.'"** (4:13-15)

You and I, as citizens of Christ's Kingdom, must not add anything to our speech with the intention that such an addition will make us more reliable or trustworthy.

Rather, we should live with unconditional integrity. Our life of holiness is sufficient evidence of the reliability of our word. Our word can be trusted because we can be trusted.

Sadly, this is not always practiced.

During a time of conflict, a local church withheld the pastor's salary check. When challenged, the treasurer stated, "Well, it's not in writing." Wow. A piece of paper with signatures has greater truth-creating power than the work of Christ in the heart?

Jesus is giving a clear call to a life of holiness. We have received a mandate to live strong and true. We are expected, and enabled, to live a life that requires no props so that we can be trusted.

Adding an oath does not give birth to truth, nor does it cause the death of falsehood. Jesus stated just the opposite. Adding an oath causes the death of truth and gives birth to falsehood. And the source of such evil is the Evil One himself.

A friend of mine goes so far as to never add "I promise" when speaking with his children. He is teaching his children that our raw word, without the prop of oaths or promises, must be enough.

May the Lord give us ears to hear the powerful simplicity of His words, words that call us to a life that gives trustworthiness to our simple 'yes' or 'no.'

Questions for reflection:

1. What value does our culture place on honesty?

2. How does our culture respond to dishonesty and lying?

3. How has this cultural perspective influenced the church?

4. How has this cultural perspective influenced your own life and practice?

5. What is your response to this statement: "Your life supports your words not the other way around"?

18. REVENGE

Our natural instinct is to push back when pushed. This push back begins early in life and only intensifies as we age. We counsel our kids to whip the bully, to not take abuse, to never start a fight but if one starts then finish it. We seem determined to send the message that if someone messes with us they are treading on dangerous ground.

Indications are given on social media that "no one can mess with me and get by with it!" Vulgarity and violence are frequent components of these messages. We buy into the delusion that strength is best expressed through being tough, defensive, vulgar and violent. "If you poke me in the eye I will break your jaw. That will show you who is the tough one!"

Mankind's history is one of feuds, skirmishes, battles, wars, murder, and violence. Most of these can be traced back to a wrong done that had to be avenged. "You punch me and I will break your arm" has been our mentality for thousands of years.

Jesus jumps into this centuries-old conversation:

> **"You have heard it said, 'Eye for eye, and tooth for tooth.' But I tell you, do not resist an evil person. If someone strikes you on the right cheek, turn to him**

the other also. And if someone wants to sue you and take your tunic, let him have your cloak as well. If someone forces you to go one mile, go with him two miles. Give to the one who asks you, and do not turn away from the one who wants to borrow from you" (vss. 38-42)

Immediately we rebel against these words. That rebellion is expressed in this story – A young man, a star athlete in High School, felt the call of God and upon graduation went away to Seminary. Upon returning to his home town some years later he encountered a former classmate. The classmate reminded the newly ordained ministry of the fights they had in their earlier days. Then he punched the preacher in the face. The preacher turned his face and took another punch. Then he removed his jacket and proceeded to thrash that classmate. When asked about his action, the preacher responded, "I only have two cheeks. After that, all bets are off."

We grin at this account and remember days when we said much the same thing. And in so doing we exercise one of our most highly developed skills - *missing the point.*

If we continue looking at the Word we will give the Spirit opportunity to make the point.

He cited the Law as recorded in **Exodus 21:23-25 –**

"But if there is serious injury, you are to take life for life, eye for eye, tooth for tooth, hand for hand, foot for foot, burn for burn, wound for wound, bruise for bruise" and in **Leviticus 24:18-20 – "If anyone injures his neighbor, whatever he has done must be done to him: fracture for fracture, eye for eye, tooth for tooth. As he has injured the other, so he is to be injured."**

Fallen nature always desires to pay back with interest. A broken tooth might result in the loss of life. This law was meant to bring personal revenge to the court and insure equal justice. It did not mandate that every single wrong had to be avenged, nor did it rule out the possibility of a lesser punishment or even an act of forgiveness.

Across the centuries this law had moved away from the mediation of the courts and priests and was allowed to be applied by individuals. This resulted in the law being used to justify personal revenge.

Jesus brings us back to the matter of the heart on this issue of revenge. In so doing He clearly and simply states: *do not strike back.* As citizens of His Kingdom we are required to abandon any rights to personal revenge.

Imagine how this must have sounded to those first listeners. They lived under oppression and abuse. Some of them had been struck just for spite. Some of them had received the insult of a back-handed slap. Many of them, if given the opportunity, would most certainly hit back with interest.

Among first century Israel existed a group of individuals known as Zealots.

> "The Zealots were members of a first-century political movement among Judean Jews who sought to overthrow the occupying Roman government. Because of their often-violent tactics, the Zealots have been called some of the world's first terrorists."[17]

According to **Luke 6:15** one of the men Jesus picked as a disciple was known as Simon the Zealot. Can you imagine how this teaching of Jesus must have sounded to Simon? To the Zealots in the crowd? To those who sympathized with the Zealots?

How does this teaching of Jesus sound to you? To me? "You mean when somebody hits me I am not allowed to hit back?" Sounds that way.

The majority of people are right handed so when Jesus states **"if someone strikes you on the right check"** He is referring to being back-handed in the face. This was a great insult meant to provoke a reaction. The closest equivalent I can think of for our culture is for someone to spit in our face. Insulting. And meant to provoke a reaction. Jesus states that the only reaction we are to

---

[17] www.gotquestions.org

give to such a degrading insult is to **"turn to him the other also."** This is a powerful statement. A back-handed slap was considered to carry twice the insult as an open-handed slap. To offer the other cheek is to show the evil person the ineffectiveness of their intended insult.

> "In that culture, the left cheek was struck with the right hand only between people who were valued as equals. So, if a person was struck backhanded on the right cheek, but then turned the left cheek to the oppressor, it sent a powerful new message. With the simple action of turning the other cheek, the powerless/inferior person has taken initiative to redefine the relationship and force the oppressor into a moral choice. The oppressor now must decide to either escalate the injustice, or admit their own bad behavior. The one oppressed, the powerless victim, now levels the playing field and is no longer the victim." [18]

As citizens in Christ's Kingdom we are to willingly risk a second blow or a second insult rather than seek personal revenge for the first. Our attitude must never be "one, two, all bets are off." We must live in submission to Christ's authority, yielding to His justice.

---

[18] Gaye Berkshire Marston, *The Truth About Me,* pg. 41.

Ancient Jewish teaching understood this portion of Christ's teaching to be about insults, not about attacks of physical violence intended to bring harm or death to family members or violent attacks against a nation as in an act of war. This teaching of Jesus was not considered a call to complete pacifism. It was a call to forego the personal right of vengeance for being insulted, however deep or painful the insult might be.

Jesus expands this teaching by instructing his listeners (and us) to go beyond the allowances of the law. When someone wants your shirt, give them the shirt and your coat. This puts the burden of law on the offender: if he keeps your coat then he stands before the judgment of God. If someone compels you to go one mile – which the Romans could demand (remember Simon who carried the cross of Christ?) – go two miles. This was not within the law and so it puts the burden of law back on the one making the demand. If someone wants to borrow, lend: this puts the burden of the law of return on them.

And in so doing we are free.

At first hearing all of this sounds like a prescription for disaster. We know all the hitters and takers who are going to take advantage of us. As soon as these evil people smell our weakness they will circle like vultures to pick us clean. If we don't stand up for ourselves we will lose everything: we will lose our dignity and our dimes. Isn't that being irresponsible? Maybe it is even bad stewardship. Don't you think God expects us to take better care of ourselves and what belongs to us? These are His gifts, His blessings, after all (and for those who lean toward health/wealth gospel, this is especially confusing).

In our near panic we forget.

We forget that we are citizens of Christ's Kingdom and as such we are under His authority, His plan, His provision, and His protection. Our only responsibility is submission to Him.

We forget that records of wrongs are not ours to keep (remember **1 Corinthians 13**?) We forget that we are not to worry about anything. We forget that we live by faith not by sight. We forget what God has declared:

> **"Do not repay anyone evil for evil. If it is possible, as far as it depends on you, live at peace with everyone. Do not take revenge, my friends, but leave room for God's wrath, for it is written, 'It is mine to avenge; I will repay,' says the Lord.'"** **(Romans 12:17-19;** see also **Deuteronomy 32:35; Hebrews 10:30-31)**

"Are you telling me that as a Christian I can't defend myself? How about defending my family? What about national defense?"

I am not the author of this passage. I, too, am grappling with the meaning and implications of this teaching of Jesus.

I took careful note that Jesus made this a personal issue. He did *not* say that when I see someone hit my wife I am to turn her cheek so she could be hit again. He did not say that when I see someone abuse my child or grandchild I am to do nothing in response. He did not say that a nation has no obligation to keep its citizens safe.

What He *did* say is that I have no right to personal revenge. That I must have a heart that is willing to be wronged, multiple times and in multiple ways, rather than react in a way that dishonors Him.

Such a life requires more strength than I have to give.

Help me Jesus.

Questions for reflection:

1. How is the idea of revenge portrayed in our culture?
TV? Movies?

2. Respond to this statement: "I only have two cheeks.
After you have hit me the second time, all bets are off!"

3. What tensions are caused by the conflict between this
teaching of Jesus and your personal ideas?

4. How is this teaching of Jesus a portrayal of strength?

5. How does this teaching need to be applied in your life
and relationships?

19. ENEMIES

Jesus told us we must not strike back when struck, that we must relinquish any rights to personal revenge. This is only possible when the supernatural life of Christ becomes natural in us through the indwelling work of the Holy Spirit.

Jesus now takes his listeners, and us, deeper into the life of holiness. It is not enough to have a neutral reaction to those who would attack or insult us:

> **"You have heard that it was said, 'Love your neighbor and hate your enemy.' But I say to you: love your enemies** (bless those that curse you)**, and pray for those who persecute you, that you may be sons of your Father in heaven. He causes his sun to rise on the evil and the good, and sends rain on the righteous and the unrighteous. If you love those who love you, what reward will you get? Are not even tax collectors doing that? And if you greet only your brothers, what are you doing more than others? Do not even pagans do that? Be perfect, therefore, as your heavenly Father is perfect."** (vss. 43-48)

The law states "**love your neighbor**" (**Leviticus 19:18**). Not everyone is my neighbor; a few people are my enemies. What do I do with those who are my enemies? Religious leaders answered that question: hate your enemies. Isn't that the unspoken implication of "love your neighbor"?

In the two records of blessing and cursing (**Leviticus 26** and **Deuteronomy 28**) God promised deliverance from enemies as part of the blessing upon obedience; part of the curse for disobedience was the pronouncement of being overcome by enemies. Prayers to God often included an appeal for deliverance from enemies or decisive victory over enemies. Enemies were not seen as opportunities to show love. Enemies were to be defeated and hated.

Luke 10 records the story we identify as "The Parable of the Good Samaritan." The story begins with an expert in the law asking Jesus about eternal life. Jesus directs this man's attention to the law in which is written **"love your neighbor as yourself." (vs. 27)** This expert, in an effort to more thoroughly understand these words of Jesus, asks, "**And who is my neighbor?**" **(vs. 29)** Jesus responds with the story of the Good Samaritan. At the end of the story Jesus asks, "**Which of the three** (priest, Levite, Samaritan) **do you think was a neighbor to the man who fell into the hands of robbers?" The expert in the law replied, "The one who had mercy on him." Jesus told him, "Go and do likewise."** (vss. 36-37)

The power of this story is found in the identity of the Samaritan. Samaritans hated and were hated by the Jews. This prejudice was deeply engrained. According to social expectations among both groups, this Samaritan should not have helped the injured man. The unspoken portion of this story tells us these two men – the Samaritan and the injured traveler – were enemies. Yet the Samaritan treated the injured man as a neighbor; according to the law the Samaritan expressed love to this stranger.

Jesus, knowing the ease with which the human heart expresses selfishness, the ease with which we take the principles of our faith and twist them to our own will and for our own purposes, draws attention to something greater than the law. He calls us to something impossible.

I think that is the point.

Jesus takes us to the heart of the matter and shows us what is the matter with our heart. He shows us that only when He rules in our heart can we ever hope to live the life of holiness to which He calls us.

"Love your enemies."

We have all seen those TV dramas when friends and relatives are asked about the murder victim: "Do you know anyone who would want to hurt your husband?" The usual answer: "He did not have any enemies." Jesus writes a different life script: He indicates that as a citizen in His Kingdom I will have enemies. Not everybody is going to love me, respect me, or even like me. As Bill Hybels reportedly said, "Not everyone will carry your picture in their wallet."

This is disturbing.

We are led to believe only good will come our way when we live the Christian life. People will come to appreciate us. Our coworkers, class mates, neighbors and family will respect us. Our growing reputation will open interesting doors of opportunity and privilege. We expect to live in the favor of the Lord and interpret that to mean favor with everybody around us. God will give us advantage even if it is at the cost of someone losing advantage: it is a Divine exchange after all – advantage taken from those who have rejected Him and given to us for our obedience. Nothing more than a polished version of Old Testament statements about enemies.

Then we discover we have been misinformed. And what should we expect? Jesus said, **"If the world hates you, keep in mind that it hated me first." (John 15:18)** Jesus further modeled the Kingdom treatment of enemies when from the cross he uttered these words: **"Father, forgive them, for they do not know what they are doing." (Luke 23:34)**

"The problem isn't having enemies. It's having the right ones and for the right reasons. Don't have enemies because you are intentionally offensive in spirit and interrelation dynamics. Don't have enemies because you are caustic and abrasive. Don't have enemies because you are unfeeling and unloving. But… Do have enemies because you stand for truth. Do have enemies because you will not waver in the face of majority opinion when it crashes against biblical authority. Do have enemies because you will not personally compromise your convictions. After all, Jesus did." [19]

How can we expect these enemies to treat us? Jesus said they would curse us and persecute us. These enemies would do nothing good toward us to cause a natural response of good back to them. Not at all. Enemies don't behave that way.

And Jesus said we are to love these people?!

How am I to express love to my enemies?

"Bless them when they curse you."

---

[19] James Emery White, *Meet Generation Z: Understanding and Reaching the New Post-Christian World,* (Grand Rapids, MI: Baker Books, 2017), pgs. 101-102.

Really? This is not even theologically sound. When an enemy curses me – an obvious display that this person is not one of God's children – I am supposed to pronounce some measure of God's favor on them? What about the whole "that which is holy to the dogs" and "pearls before swine" thing? Doesn't that apply here? Wouldn't pronouncing some blessing on such a person allow them to believe God loves them?

Have you ever tried this? After someone has given you a good cussing – or expressed some ill and harm upon you – have you ever looked at them and said, "I wish only the best for you. I hope you experience the blessing of God on your life today."?

This is not possible. I don't want to do this. I'm not sure I can even fake it.

Unless, of course, holiness is at work in me.

"Pray for those who persecute you."

After someone has done something painful, devastating, destructive, maybe even tragic, we are to pray for them.

I don't want to pray for them. Unless it is in the Old Testament style:

> **"May his children be fatherless and his wife a widow. May his children be wandering beggars; may they be driven from their ruined homes. May**

no one extend kindness to him or take pity on his fatherless children. May his sins always remain before the LORD, that He may cut off the memory of them from the earth" (yes that is real; see **Psalm 109**).

Several years ago, someone did our daughter a terrible wrong. I was angered by the event. Daddy's girl cried for three days and I was ready to take action in a strong and violent way. God interrupted my morning prayers: "Would you like to get past this?" Yes, of course. "Pray for them." I began praying like the verses cited above. God interrupted me again: "Not really what I had in mind." I had to first be cleansed and then pray for those who had wronged our daughter. And I found peace.

If we pray for those who wrong us with the intent Jesus would approve, that would be the one prayer God will surely answer. Can you imagine *that* person becoming a brother or sister in Christ!

My own unholiness is becoming more obvious with each moment.

Jesus makes my unholiness undeniable: He makes God the Father the standard for the treatment of enemies.

Not some good person. Not some saintly Christian. Nope.

God Himself.

We tend to love those who love us and to greet only those who greet us. There is nothing special, nothing Kingdom, about that. Anyone can live to that standard.

But God? Watch the rain of the next spring shower. It will rain on your sanctified garden over which you have prayed a great blessing. And it will rain on your neighbor's marijuana patch. Watch the sun as it shines. It will shine on your carefully manicured lawn and on your neighbor's overgrown, weed-infested mess.

God shows providential care in equal measure to His enemies and His children.

I don't like it and certainly don't understand it. I like it even less that God behaves is such a way and announces: "Do the same thing. Treat your enemies and your neighbors with the same measure of unbiased kindness."

Can't. Do. It.

Not by discipline. Not by personality. Not by faking it.

The ability to love my enemies will only happen when I share in the very nature of God. The nature of God that comes to dwell in me by the sanctifying work of the Holy Spirit.

I think I need to pray.

Questions for reflection:

1. What does our culture say we should do about an enemy?

2. How is that cultural value expressed?

3. What influence has this cultural value had upon the church?

4. What has been your personal response to an enemy?

5. What difference(s), if any, needs to be made to your attitude and actions toward your enemy?

6. How is that change to be accomplished?

20. DOING GOOD
Matthew 6

For a number of years, I have been uncomfortable whenever a public display is made of personal giving. It was, and still is, the way money is raised in many church settings. I well remember the "pledge time" of camp meetings and revivals. Those times were torture for a young boy. On and on and on in a predictable pattern: "Who will give $1,000? $500? $200? $100? $50? $20?" Most of the time the needed money was raised and since the pledge time worked it continued year after year in the same tortuous event.

One moment stands out in my memory. Public pledges were being taken for a special project. During that time of appeal, a local church came on the platform carrying a check the size of a banner. That check announced the donation amount from that local church to the project. The room erupted in applause. I wanted to be anywhere else in that moment. There were certainly a large number of right and left hands that knew what they were doing as they struck each other in applause.

There has always been something in our nature that wants to be recognized for our good deeds, that wants to announce – "Now, I'm *not* bragging, but..." The people on the hill listening to this Teacher were plagued by the same twist of character. All of us want to be seen as people who do good. We are secretly hopeful the public display of good will be translated to mean we are good. We desire to be applauded for our show but not known in those quiet recesses of the heart. In spite of our best expressions of faith-alone-by-grace- alone doctrine, we continue to display our righteousness before the eyes of men.

Jesus continues what he has so skillfully been doing: he gets past the show to the very heart of the matter:

> **"Be careful not to do your 'acts of righteousness' before men, to be seen by them. If you do, you will have no reward from your Father in heaven. So when you give to the needy, do not announce it with trumpets, as the hypocrites do in the synagogue and on the streets, to be honored by men. I tell you the truth, they have received their reward in full. But when you give to the needy, do not let your left hand know what your right hand is doing, so that you giving may be in secret. Then your Father, who sees what is done in secret, will reward you."** (vss. 1-4)

Motivation.

Motivations are decided in the hidden place of the heart. This is both encouraging and cautionary. Encouraging in that we need not announce or try to persuade others concerning our motivations: such an attempt would seem contrary to the teaching of Christ. Cautionary in that God knows the heart: no possibility of deception or hypocrisy.

Here is a question that helps discern if our motivations are selfish or righteous: "Am I doing this out of my concern for my standing before others? Am I simply trying to build a good reputation?" Or try this one: "If I were certain that no one would ever know about this good deed would I still do it?" If we are really feeling bold: "Will I be offended if no one says 'thank you'?"

Questions like these tend to expose our motivations. Jesus makes one thing abundantly clear – if we perform good deeds with the hope of receiving anything from people we have already received our reward in full. If we do a good deed to enhance our reputation or build our resume, our reward will be in the reputation or resume. If we do a good deed in hopes people will define us as good, we have received our reward. If we do a good deed to receive a 'thank you,' when thanks is given we have our payday.

Most of the time it is a pitiful payday. Most of the time it is a payday that must be repeated again and again: we train ourselves to live from payday to payday. One more applause. A little more appreciation. Another note of thanks. And we are fueled to do another good deed.

I was standing in an area thrift shop and overhearing two ladies talking. I felt awkward even though these two were making no effort at being private in their conversation. One was recounting the cards and expressions of good will they had extended again and again to a particular person. Evidently the receiving person did not return the kindnesses. "Why should I be the one to always reach out and be kind? If they are not going to at least acknowledge my good deed, then I'm done." And so the conversation went for several minutes. It was a small moment which reflected the big picture of how most of us feel when our good deeds go unrecognized. At first my own heart was nodding in agreement: why waste a good deed on a thankless person?

One of the problems with such an approach is this: we give the other person the power to determine if we do a good deed. Rather than living in obedience to an expressed principle of the Kingdom we are now living as victims of the whims of another person. If they will, then we will; if they won't, then we won't.

That attitude is a carnal virus that will soon infect more than our doing of good deeds.

Let's not allow confusion or selfishness to move us to inactivity. Jesus expects that our good deeds be seen: **"Let your light so shine before men, that they may see**

**your good deeds and praise your Father in heaven."
(Matthew 5:16)**

Our good deeds, deeds seen and known by others, are to be motivated by a desire to bring glory to God.

Recently a young man said to me, "I don't know why I have to worry about what other people think of me." In my answer I attempted to reflect the principle of this verse. The opinion of another person has no impact upon my standing before God. Even so, the opinion of another person about me *as a Christian* may have an impact on their perspective of God. Being seen and known as a person who does good, especially good as described by the principles of the Sermon on the Mount, will cause a person to think a certain way about me. As a result, their thoughts about God will be affected as well. So yes, I should care what people think of me but only as it relates to God receiving the glory.

I have heard individuals say, "I love helping people." I appreciate such an expression of kindness. The world would be a better place if more people had such an attitude.

Even so, such a motivation falls short of that to which Christ calls us. In the concealed places of the heart our motivation must be singularly exclusive: to the glory of God alone.

Just as we are to relinquish any rights to personal revenge, as citizens within Christ's Kingdom we are to release all expectations of reward. We do good for the glory of God alone. Doing good for the reward tarnishes that good with selfishness.

> "Since Christlikeness is my magnificent obsession, I work to know how my life looks to Jesus and duplicate what He would do in my circumstances. I want to go where Jesus would go if He lived in my neighborhood or town. I want to say what Jesus would say to people in my relationships, both intimate and professional. I want to give the way Jesus would give to the needs around me. This effort to be Christlike in all levels of living makes me more like Him and helps me serve others the way He served. Service, as it calls me to wholehearted Christlikeness, challenges my attitudes about self and others... My intentional caring for others is God's cure for my me-firstism. All this adds up to another miracles and mystery about service – the more I do for Christ, the more I really do believe He is the Savior of the world." [20]

---

[20] Neil B. Wiseman, *The Untamed God: Unleashing the Supernatural in the Body of Christ,* (Kansas City, MO: Beacon Hill Press, 1997), pgs. 134, 135.

Doing good is a necessary part of being a citizen of the Kingdom of Christ, but no amount of doing good will ever move us from unprofitable servant to a servant worthy of reward.

The day is never coming when God will convene a heavenly council meeting to announce: "Todd has done enough good to pass from 'debtor' to 'profitable.' See to it that the official records make note of this change in status and reward Todd accordingly."

Not going to happen. In spite of the culturally-driven redefinition of Christianity. I encounter this redefinition over and over. I have conducted numerous pre-marriage counsel sessions during my pastoral ministry. At some point I always ask: "If someone walked up to you and asked, 'Are you a Christian?' how would you answer?" All but once I have been given the answer, "Yes." I follow up with this question: "What if that same person then asked, 'How can you make such a claim?' how would you answer?" All but once the answer followed the same path: "I try to be a good person and do good for others." We have been deceived into believing by the doing of good we neutralize or at least counterbalance the bad. In other words, we believe we can become profitable: that our good will outweigh our bad.

We are not worthless servants. The good we do *is* good. When it is motivated by the glory of God alone we can embrace this grand promise: **"Always give yourselves**

fully to the work of the Lord, because you know that your work in the Lord is never wasted." (**1 Corinthians 15:58** NCV)

Worthless servants? Never. The good we do in the Lord's service and to His glory is never a waste, never worthless.

Unprofitable servants? Yes: how could we ever reach the point of no longer being indebted to grace?

I am grateful.

Jesus states that we must not let our left hand know what our right hand is doing. Anybody else ever squint when you read those words? What could He mean?

Here is what I think – we are to do good for others so easily, so consistently, with such pure motive, that we are actually forgetful of our own actions. In some mysterious way our own good works are concealed even from us. We do good and do not think to give ourselves applause. Our hearts have been so cleansed by the presence of the Holy Spirit that our hands have no thought to clap our own applause.

If the right and left hand are unaware of each other how could they ever coordinate together for self-applause?

Could that be part of the element of surprise expressed in **Matthew 25**? You remember the story: Jesus announces blessing upon those who ministered to Him when he was in need. "When did we see you in need and minister to you?" They did not reply; "Oh, yeah. I remember that time when I helped you. I was wondering if anybody noticed."

There is great beauty and deep peace in the forgetfulness of pure motives.

Such purity of motive does not come naturally. Jesus was, and still is, quite aware of the condition of the human heart. Only by the ongoing sanctifying presence of the Holy Spirit can we have the glory of God as our only motive for doing good.

That is the way things work in the Kingdom of Christ.

Questions for reflection

1. How does our culture value the idea of self-applause?

2. How many examples can you think of that show self-applause?

3. How many examples are you willing to acknowledge from your own life?

4. Respond to this statement: "There is great beauty and deep peace in the forgetfulness of pure motives."

21. IN THE CENTER...

Christ's teaching on prayer falls in the middle of the Sermon on the Mount. Our Lord is too wise for this to be anything but intentional. I feel, very keenly, the need for prayer. I desire to be a true citizen in Christ's Kingdom. I trust you are experiencing the same sense of deep conviction. The teachings of the Kingdom still ahead of us can only be embraced by a heart conditioned by prayer.

Even in the kingdom of this world prayers are prayed. Pagans pray to their god(s). The godless pray – or at least ask for prayer on Facebook whenever faced with real difficulty. Religious people pray. A show of prayer is often made as part of public and political events. There is a profusion of prayer being made every day all over the world.

Americanized Christianity teaches us to pray under the shadows of the American dream. We pray for prosperity. Most of us have seen those Facebook posts, complete with a meme of money, stating "type 'Amen,' share and like and you will be blessed." We participate in materialistic prayer when we type 'Amen.' We pray for our individual needs, often oblivious to the larger needs of community and to the consequences an answer to our individualistic prayer might have on that community. We pray for personal success. We pray for experiences of pleasure and happiness. We pray with the good life as our motivation and our goal.

We have developed strange ideas about prayer. Some think we must pray out loud. If twenty people gather for prayer and remain in silence for an hour and go home, then six people gather for prayer and raise the roof, inevitably the second prayer gathering is considered the better prayer time. Some go so far as to accuse others of not praying at all if they pray in silence.

We have developed unnatural vocal habits when we pray. I have vivid memories from my childhood of congregational prayer. At one church such prayer was loud and fervent. One man spent the time uttering loud groans. Others prayed in a voice that was not natural to their normal communication. I began to pray with a high-pitched voice, somehow confused into believing such prayer was more likely to be heard, or at least that such prayer expressed the sincerity of my heart.

Sometimes we use special prayer language. For some that means they are going to pray in 'tongues.' For others it means they are going to pray in the language of the King James Version of the Bible. I remember one college professor who prayed like he taught: in outline form.

The position of the body is considered critical. Kneeling in prayer is the most sacred position. Being seated during prayer is almost a sacrilege. Standing for prayer is just OK. Face down on the floor is the most intense posture. There are those who believe the position of the body is a reflection of the condition of the heart.

We are persuaded that we must close our eyes when we pray. *Why?* I remember being part of a group of believers in Israel and the leader praying – standing, looking up...with his eyes open! I must confess: all the years of tradition made me a bit uncomfortable at first. Then I had a sense of embarrassment. It was though I was a voyeur listening to a private conversation between the most intimate of friends. I closed my eyes, not to enhance the holiness of the moment, but in an attempt to hide my own unholiness. I weep still as I remember that moment.

Even though most of these habits are well intended, by our manipulations of prayer we have sterilized the event. Prayer is no longer in touch with pain, trauma, the ravages of sin, and the cruel deceptions of the enemy. We no longer sully prayer in the trenches of warfare. And these prayers have become ritual, liturgical, detached and meaningless.

As a result the church prayer meeting died.

Rightly so.

When prayer takes on the form of ritual, when prayer becomes a function of self-prescribed righteousness, when prayer is a form of religion devoid of power or passion, it becomes a deceptive tool of delusion. We will claim a prayer life where neither prayer nor life exist. The more deeply entrenched such a habit becomes the further we are removed from the vitality of true prayer.

Jesus gives us a simple, yet incomprehensibly profound, prescription for prayer. We will spend a few pages just dusting the surface and a life time exploring the possibilities.

> "Prayer does bring, even to the busiest and most harassed minds, a clearer insight, a calmer judgement, a re-orientation of the mind to its true alignments. And if Jesus found this a rewarding gift of God, how much more precious would it be for our perplexed and burdened thoughts. In His case it was but the return to the mind's normal centre (sic) of rest, in God: in ours, it has more the aspect of daily divine guidance, and the gift of understanding what the will of the Lord is. But however we define and analyse (sic) – how much we need it! Yet the peace of Christ is neither fatalistic, like the Mohammedan's, nor merely negative like the Buddhist's, nor proudly indifferent like the Stoic's. It is the peace that can either ride the storm or end it, when He comes upon the lake from a mountain-top prayer. He can be silent before Herod, commanding before Pilate,

dignified before the shouting crowd, gracious even on the cross, because He has wrestled in Gethsemane alone. Truly, in His communion with God He found a secret that has eluded all men everywhere – save those who have sat at His feet – the secret of the restful soul that finds its strength in deep serenity and its power in stillness of the spirit. We do not need the advice of the psychiatrist, nor the warnings of the surgeon, to bring home to us our need of inward restfulness. Our hearts cry for it." [21]

---

[21] Reginald E. O. White, *They Teach Us To Pray,* (New York: Harper and Brothers Publishers, 1957), pgs. 193, 194.

22. WHEN YOU PRAY

Ours is not the first time in history when the practice of prayer has been twisted, tarnished and neglected. Jesus comes directly to the issue:

> **"And when you pray, do not be like the hypocrites, for they love to pray standing in the synagogues and on the street corners to be seen by men. I tell you the truth, they have received their reward in full. But when you pray, go into your room, close the door and pray to your Father, who is unseen. Then your Father, who sees what is done in secret, will reward you. And when you pray, do not keep babbling like pagans, for they think they will be heard because of their many words. Do not be like them, for your Father knows what you need before you ask him."** (vss. 5-8)

Prayer was a part of daily life. A call to prayer was sounded in the morning and in the evening. When that call was sounded it was not unusual for people to pray where they happened to be at the time. Religious leaders and the hypocrites made sure they were in a very public place when the call to prayer was sounded. These hypocrites would then say lengthy prayers (**Mark 12:40**) as a matter of performance. They desired to become known as men of prayer without ever truly seeking conversation with the Father. Since their motive was to be seen and heard by men, being seen and heard by men was their reward in full.

Jesus calls his people, the citizens of his Kingdom, to a different method of prayer with a different motive for prayer.

Jesus teaches the necessity and the value of personal prayer: prayer that happens within the concealed places of the heart. The heart is the place where there can be no pretense, no hypocrisy: a place protected from all carnal attempts at making an impression. The heart is the place where prayer is *real*, where prayer contends. A place free from the allure of applause, a place to be emptied and to be filled, and a place that is not limited by geography, body position, or external conditions.

The heart is the place to be alone with the Father.

In that holy place – alone with the Father – there is no need for thoughtless repetitions. In that holy place – alone with the Father – there is no reason to believe that added hours improve or impress the audience. In that holy place – alone with the Father – increased volume does not increase the hearing.

In that holy place – alone with the Father – the heart is exposed. Not only ours: the heart of the Father is also revealed.

In that place of knowing and being known something beyond ritual takes place.

Relational intimacy happens.

God is my Father and I am His child.

This relational intimacy, this knowing and being known, does not happen any other way.

Bible reading, gathering for worship, fellowship with other believers, receiving the sacraments, all have mysterious value beyond our grasp. These are empty without the relational intimacy of prayer. Prayer elevates those disciplines to the realm of devotion: we love the Father, we know the Father, we are loved and known by the Father, which moves us to read His Letter to us, to offer Him our adoration, to celebrate Him with family, and to gladly receive His supply of grace.

To neglect this relational intimacy is to act as orphans. Practicing such neglect is to invite the loneliness, the despair, the want, the pain, the fear, the uncertainty that marks the life of an orphan child.

 Neglecting relational intimacy is to forget *we have a Father who already knows.*

"Prayer is not getting things from God; prayer is getting into perfect communion with God; I tell Him what He knows in order that I may get to know it as He does. Pray because you have a Father..." [22]

Jesus, teach us to pray as to a Father who already knows!

As parents we already know certain things about the needs of our children. We know they need adequate shelter, protection from harm (both real and imaginary), nutritious food, appropriate clothing, specialized care when sick or hurting, education, love...the list is long but not unknown to a good parent. It would be a strange relationship, maybe even an abusive one, if our kids felt they were required to ask if they could stay indoors at night, or if they could take a seat at the table for supper, or if we had noticed holes in their socks or underwear. Even though they should never have to ask such questions we still want to have conversation with them. We want that conversation so that we can build a relationship. We want to hear about their day, their dreams, and their stories. We want to share our history, our experiences, our hopes and our dreams for them. We desire to blend their stories with our stories and through that blending create a beautiful life.

Jesus leaned into this when he said,

---

[22] Oswald Chambers, *Studies in the Sermon on the Mount*, (Grand Rapids, MI: Discovery House Publishers, 1995), pg. 58.

"Which of your fathers, if your son asks for a fish, will give him a snake instead? Or if he asks for an egg, will give him a scorpion? If you then, though you are evil, know how to give good gifts to your children, how much more will your Father in heaven give the Holy Spirit to those who ask him!" (Luke 11:11-13)

It has been my experience that when I pray simply and directly to God as Father, He answers. Many years ago, during the time of my first pastoral tenure, I was in dire need of work boots. I had no money for such a purchase. One morning I simply asked: "Lord, you know I need work boots and cannot buy them." I went to work in the stock room at the local Sears store and saw a pair of work boots sitting on top of the catalogue return bin. I asked the lady in charge of the catalogue department about them: "I cannot give them to you but I can sell them to you for $1." On another occasion I needed tires on the car. Again, I had no means to buy them so I simply prayed, "Lord you know I need tires but have no means to buy them." Within days a friend asked if I would be offended if he gave me a set of good used tires. Two sentence-prayers and two dramatic answers.

The Sunday after Thanksgiving, 2016, I was admitted to the local hospital with a hemorrhaging ulcer (I learned later that I was just a couple of days from bleeding to death). The ulcer was caused by the constant use of aspirin/ibuprofen products. I had been having headaches for a couple of years and the only effective treatment was a combination of NSAID/ibuprofen and caffeine. The doctor was explicit: *no more NSAIDs.* Ever. That night I had a massive headache that morphine did not treat successfully. I was concerned about my ability to function once released from the hospital. I prayed: "As a son to a Father, I ask you to take my headaches away." I am blessed to tell you the Father heard me and answered by taking my headaches away for several months.

Prayer, real prayer, is not meant to inform God of our needs. He already knows our needs far more accurately than we ever could. Have we forgotten God is the God of all knowledge? Have we forgotten God is intimately aware of what is going on in the lives of His children? Have we forgotten that the circumstances and situations that intersect with our lives must first pass by the throne of our Father? Whatever our request, however urgently we are pressed by the burden, we will never surprise the Father with our petition.

Prayer, real prayer, is not meant to persuade a God who is reluctant to respond. He already knows the plan he has for us, the path designated for us, and has already made every provision for the successful completion of our journey. We are mistaken if we believe our prayers interrupt the busy-ness of God in such a way as to force Him to alter His activity and give attention to us and our need. *God is with us.* By His Holy Spirit He is in us. He is the one constant of our journey. The finiteness of our senses in no way gives us an accurate perception of the work of the Father. The Word gives us a sure foundation for our faith: God is our Father, He is present, and He is continually at work.

Prayer is a declaration of love. Prayer is an affirmation of our dependence upon the Father. Prayer is a statement of trust that the Father will only do what is right and good for his children. Prayer declares our faith in the constancy of the Father's involvement. Prayer is not the attempt to win a response: prayer is the heart's surrender to the presence of the Father. Prayer is the recognition that apart from relational intimacy all else simply becomes religion.

Jesus teaches us how to express our love, our dependence and our desire for relational intimacy in what we often refer to as, "The Lord's Prayer."

Read on with a prayerful heart.

Questions for reflection:

1. Our culture often views prayer as a one-way communication: we talk to God but must never claim that God speaks to us. How has such a perspective influenced your view of prayer?

2. In what ways have prayer habits actually weakened what prayer is meant to be?

3. Recount a time in your life when a simple prayer received a dramatic answer.

4. Respond to this statement: "To neglect this relational intimacy is to act as orphans. Practicing such neglect is to invite the loneliness, the despair, the want, the pain, the fear, the uncertainty that marks the life of an orphan child."

23. OUR FATHER

Jesus finished describing the prayer practices of hypocrites and pagans: public display for the attention of men and the use of lengthy, babbling prayers. He presents these as ways we must not pray.

Now Jesus makes this simple statement: **"This, then, is how you should pray…"**

For all the sermons preached, Sunday School classes taught, and volumes written about prayer, it comes down to a model for prayer that is less than seventy-five words.

Jesus, the only Begotten of the Father, should know how to talk to the Father: we would do well to learn from this simple, yet profound, model for prayer. The ease with which we memorize these words must not deceive us as to the profound depths of the truths contained.

"Our Father in heaven, hallowed be your name." (vs. 9)

The title "father" does not always bring up the best of thoughts. Far too many earthly fathers do not merit the title; through abuse, selfishness, abandonment and a multitude of other offenses they prove themselves less than a father. I have heard story after story from adult children describing the pains of growing up with such a father. These stories expose deep scars from past pains that make a present relationship with anyone titled "father" a near impossibility. Can you imagine closing such a conversation with an invitation to talk to Father God? Such a scarred and hurting person would approach God with terror; with the expectation that God was going to criticize, belittle, and attack; that in some way this Father God was going to add to the pain and misery of life or ignore them completely.

Other fathers failed in their duties by indulgence and permissiveness. These fathers never set and enforced boundaries upon their children. Those children are aptly known as brats, made so by the failures of their father. Those children grow up to become entitled, narcissistic adults. They hold the world to a ruthless standard and themselves to none.

Some churches are full of such adults. Watch them as the preacher promises great financial blessings and materialistic miracles. Cheering, shouting, standing applause. Such a person will approach Father God as a limitless resource of indulgence.

Neither approach to Father God will work. Neither of these approaches to Father God is what Jesus is instructing when he says, **"This, then, is how you should pray: 'Father...'"**

Yet the question remains: how can we pray to God as Father when earthly fatherhood is so marred by sin?

We must turn to a Biblical definition of the Father. With time, and the help of this Father, we can separate our experiences of earthly fathers from the Biblical definitions of the heavenly Father. Faith in this Father can replace the failures of all other fathers.

Only then can we learn to effectively embrace this model prayer presented by Jesus.

We can trust the record about the Heavenly Father. Scripture tells us that God, as Father, desires to give good gifts (and the Holy Spirit) to any who would ask (see **Matthew 7:11; Luke 11:13**). Scripture also tells us that God, as Father, disciplines us for our good:

> **"'My son, do not make light of the Lord's discipline, and do not lose heart when he rebukes you, because the Lord disciplines those he loves, and he punishes everyone he accepts as a son.' God disciplines us for our good, that we may share in his holiness." (Hebrews 12:5-6, 10)**

God, as Father, loves us with a crazy love: **"How great is the love the Father has lavished on us, that we should be called children of God!" (1 John 3:1)**

What comes to mind when you hear that the Father "lavishes his love on us"?

I see God, as Father, taking a huge bucket and filling it to overflowing with *agape*. He then calls over a few angels: "See my son? He has forgotten how much I love him. I think now is a good time to remind him, don't you?" With a broad grin He then dumps the entire bucket on me. I am completely saturated. I am momentarily blinded by the deluge. I cough and sputter. Even the ground all around me is soaked. Everything yields to that moment. My plans are entirely rearranged. Nothing about me is unaffected.

Lavished love has that effect.

Less than one minute before giving us a model for prayer, Jesus gave us a definition of the Father: **"the Father knows what you need before you ask him."**

The Bible would have us understand that God, as Father, is generous, involved, lavish in His love, and knows our need.

Surely you and I can talk to a Father like that.

That being said, Jesus giving this model for prayer is not about experiencing God in some emotional, feel-good way. God, as Father, is not to be seen as some cosmic version of a really good earthly father. We cannot reduce God, the Father, to one who is responsible to serve us for our self-defined good. Prayer is not, and cannot be devolved into, that which manipulates the Father to do our will.

Neither is prayer to be seen as a weak attempt to appease an angry God, or to delay the inevitable punishment coming from a severely disappointed God.

The listeners of the first century would never have interpreted this model prayer in any of these ways.

When these Jewish first listeners heard Jesus tell them to pray by addressing God as "Father," their minds made an immediate journey across hundreds of years to a time when God declared them as His son and He their Father (see **Exodus 4:22**) and changed their national status from slave to sons.

The people of Israel – delivered as slaves and adopted as sons – viewed God as Father, not just for intimacy of relationship but for revolution; not just for familiarity, but for hope. This Father God is the One who delivered them with a mighty hand; He is the One who broke the tyrant's grip; He is the One who set them free; He is the One who guided them; He is the One who provided them with an entirely new manner of living. He is the One who provided the Great Exodus. He is the One they remembered in their songs, their feasts, and their celebrations. He is the One who would send the Messiah and bring about another Exodus, a new Exodus, and once again deliver them, break the tyrant's grip, and set them free.

To call this God "Father" was to remember the ancient Exodus and to hope for the renewal of the promises in a New Exodus.

For us, when we pray "our Father," we are not just addressing some nice guy in the sky. Jesus is teaching us to remember the One who delivered us, who broke the tyrant's grip, who set us free, who guides us and gives us a new manner of living; the One who did for us what we were powerless to do for ourselves. He is teaching us to remember God's past actions with praise, observe His present action with hope, and look for His future action with faith.

Those first listeners understood yet another powerful nuance in the words "our Father." In ancient Israel, even in the days of Jesus, the son learned the trade of the father. Jesus was known as the son of a carpenter and was himself trained by Joseph in the arts of carpentry. From an early age a son would imitate his father until he learned to do what the father did.

When Jesus said, "Start praying by saying 'Father'" (in the original language the word 'father' is the first word) those first listeners were startled by the implications. From their cultural understanding of the title "father" they heard these unspoken words: consider yourself, in relation to God as Father, an apprentice. Know that prayer begins with a desire to imitate the Father, to learn to do what the Father is doing. Listen to these words of

Jesus that imply apprenticeship: **"I do nothing on my own but speak just what the Father has taught me. I am telling you what I have seen in the Father's presence, …"** (**John 8:28,38**) The writer to the Hebrews made this intense statement: **"Although he** (Jesus) **was a son, he learned obedience from what he suffered…."** (5:8) The words of N. T. Wright are fitting here:

> "We, too, need to learn what it means to call God 'Father', and we mustn't be surprised by what it means. Saying 'our father' isn't just boldness, the sheer cheek of walking into the presence of the living and almighty God and saying, 'Hi, Dad.' It is the boldness, the sheer total risk, of saying quietly, 'Please may I, too, be considered an apprentice son.'" [23]

To pray, **"Our Father,"** is to sign an application for apprenticeship. These words express a desire, an intention, to listen, to watch, and to imitate the Father until we learn to do what He does.

This is no strange consideration. Jesus tells us to be as the Heavenly Father in our treatment of others, even our enemies (see **Matthew 6:43-48**). After Jesus washed the feet of the disciples he instructs them to imitate him (see

---

[23] N. T. Wright, *The Lord and His Prayer,* (Grand Rapids, MI: William B. Eerdmans Publishing Company, 1996), pg. 8.

John 13). The Apostle Paul boldly states, **"Follow my example, as I follow the example of Christ."** (**1 Corinthians 11:1**). In **1 John** we are told that since Christ laid down his life for us we should lay down our lives for each other (**3:16**) and since God loves us we should love one another (**4:11**).

When we pray, **"Our Father,"** we are remembering the One in whom all our hope rests; He was our hope in the past, He is our hope in the present and continues to be our hope as we move into the future.

When we prayer, **"Our Father,"** we are making an astonishing, crazy, and utterly risky claim: we intend to learn to do what God is doing; we will watch, learn and listen in the presence of the Father so that we can stand in the presence of the sin, darkness, pain and despair of our world – His world – as His light, as His witness, as His words.

The Father is identified as **"in heaven."** The ancient Jews believed heaven was God's dwelling place and the earth was man's dwelling place. They considered these two places as distinct but not as far distant and disconnected. It was believed that heaven and earth intersected at various times and in various ways. When God spoke to Abram, when Moses encountered the burning bush, when the children of Israel followed the pillar of cloud and when Moses received the Law, these were all considered times when heaven and earth intersected.

The most sacred intersection of heaven and earth occurred at the Temple. This is why a pilgrimage was made to the Temple each year. This is why Jews looked to the Temple when they prayed. This is why the Temple held such a protected and sacred place in the life of Israel. This is why the destruction of the Temple became an issue in the trial of Jesus.

The first century Jews embraced the belief of heaven and earth intersecting in Torah. Those who read and lived by Torah were in the presence of God as though they were at the Temple.

When Jesus instructs his listeners to pray to the Father in heaven, he is not asking them to pray to some far distant, disconnected Deity. He is not even asking them to long for heaven. He is reminding them of their history and those times when heaven and earth intersected. He is reminding them that at various times and in various places, with little pattern or prediction, heaven and earth joined as God's presence mingled with humanity. This fills the hearts of the first listeners with anticipation: the God to whom they pray might cause His presence to be known right here, right now, so He must be very near.

This truth is a beautiful consideration.

This Heavenly Father's name is a Holy name. The Jews considered the name of God as given to Moses at the burning bush so holy that they refused to speak it or write it. Isaiah declared the LORD as **"Holy, Holy, Holy"** **(Isaiah 6:3)**. John tells us of four living creatures around the throne of God declaring day and night **"Holy, Holy, Holy is the LORD God Almighty" (Revelation 4:8)**. Holiness is the only aspect of the character and nature of God that is ever emphasized by a triplicate declaration: **"Holy, Holy, Holy."**

> "Holiness is the characteristic of God's nature that is at the very core of His being. Only as we encounter God in His holiness is it possible for us to see ourselves as we really are. The view of God presented in Isaiah 6:1-4 leaves an individual with a deep sense of awe at the greatness of His majesty. To be indifferent is impossible for the Christian when confronted with the holiness of God." [24]

Some Jews yet today will not write out "God" but will write "G-d." This discipline is a constant reinforcement of the holiness of the name of God. His name, His identity, is not to be taken lightly.

Even in prayer.

Especially in prayer.

---

[24] R.C. Sproul, *the Holiness of God*, Study Guide, (Orlando, FL: Ligonier Ministries Curriculum Series, 1988), pg. 15.

This example of how to open a time of prayer disallows flippant attitudes, careless posturing, and foolish petitions. It serves to position us in proper relation to the God of heaven Who is Holy, Holy, Holy and at the same time our Father. It allows us to see Him more clearly: no person who has ever seen God as Holy, Holy, Holy and as Father can possibly remain unaware of their own personal unholiness and their own unworthiness to be a son or daughter of this God.

Starting prayer in this manner is a reinforcement of these Beatitudes: **"Blessed are the poor in spirit...are those who mourn...are the meek."**

May the Holy Spirit stop our headlong rush into prayer. We all benefit by breathing in the transforming power of such a start to prayer.

Remember, Jesus said **"This, then, is how you should pray."**

Questions for reflection:

1. How does our culture view the idea of fatherhood?

2. How has that idea impacted the idea of God being a Father?

3. How does your personal experience impact viewing God as Father?

4. How does the idea of the nearness of heaven to earth change your thinking about prayer?

5. How are you challenged by the holiness of the name of God?

24. YOUR KINGDOM COME

"This, then, is how you should pray...your kingdom come, your will be done on earth as it is in heaven." (vs. 10)

There are those who declare this sentence a "Millennial Prayer." By that they mean this portion of the Lord's Prayer is aimed at the one-thousand-year millennial reign of Christ as interpreted from **Revelation 20.**

That perspective is disturbing to me for a few reasons:

>the first listeners to whom this model prayer was presented had no real working concept of the millennium reign of Jesus as interpreted by modern-day dispensationalists (remember - at the time of the Sermon on the Mount the **Revelation** had not yet been given).

>how could the first listeners understand and accurately define or apply this Prayer as a whole if parts of it are for right now, parts to be applied later, and some parts refer to some far-off distant future beyond their own lives?

>would Jesus really "leap-frog" over these first listeners to some group of readers several centuries into the future?

>would Jesus really teach these first listeners to pray a prayer that had no possibility of answer in their own lifetime?

We are closer to understanding the teachings of Jesus –
including this prayer - when we remember Jesus and His
listeners are influenced by certain points of reference
available at the time: the Torah, the Prophets and the
established traditions of the Jewish people.

This sentence prayer about the Kingdom is better understood
as a right-here, right-now, already-but-not-yet kind of prayer.

The people of Israel understood the Kingdom this way.

For the people of Israel, the Kingdom was understood to be
an earthly, social, political reality over which God, through
the Messiah, would rule as King in righteousness, holiness,
and justice.

Daniel 7:13-14 is one of the Hebrew Scriptures about the
Kingdom with which Jesus and this first audience were
familiar:

> **"In my vision at night I looked, and there before me
> was one like a son of man, coming with the clouds
> of heaven. He approached the Ancient of Days and
> was led into his presence. He was given authority,
> glory and sovereign power; all peoples, nations and
> men of every language worshiped him. His
> dominion is an everlasting dominion that will not
> pass away, and his kingdom is one that will never be
> destroyed."**

We must not overlook the connection between these verses in Daniel and the following words of the Risen Christ: **"All authority in heaven and earth has been given to me" (Matthew 28:18)**.

The Apostle Paul echoes the words of Daniel after describing the humble obedience of Christ:

> **"There God exalted him to the highest place and gave him the name that is above every name, that at the name of Jesus every knee should bow, in heaven and on earth and under the earth, and every tongue confess that Jesus Christ is Lord, to the glory of God the Father" (Philippians 2:9-11)**.

Throughout the Old Testament the Kingdom of God is never a Kingdom waiting for a particular point in time. It is a Kingdom interacting with and through the Jewish people as it anticipates the coming of a Person in time. That person is Jesus. In Jesus the Kingdom is portrayed in its fullness and established as already-but-not-yet.

Jesus presented the Kingdom of God as a right-here, right-now, already-but-not-yet Kingdom.

The Kingdom is the common thread binding the preaching and parables of Jesus together. It is His most consistent theme. As you read the account of **Matthew**, Jesus repeatedly treats the Kingdom as a right-here, right-now, already Kingdom (see **4:23; 6:33; 9:35; 10:7; 11:12; 12:28; 16:19,28**).

In **Matthew 8:11** and **26:29** He also speaks of the Kingdom in terms of the not-yet future. He treats the Kingdom as a present reality awaiting its final consummation.

The Kingdom was never understood by the Jews, or by Jesus, as something separated from the present day, as something separated from the world of space, time and matter.

This historical understanding of the Kingdom gives great insight into the motivation and intentionality of this prayer. Language about the Kingdom was not just some poetic way of acknowledging God as God or expressing a longing for a great by-and-by. Prayers for the coming of the Kingdom of God are not meant to promote an escapist mentality, with all of its potential neglects and abuses.

By including the Kingdom in this model prayer, Jesus intends to stir memory, give hope, urge participation and fill with anticipation.

By the first century, for over six hundred years the Jews had been longing for a New Exodus, for a time when their God would once again manifest His rule, once again enforce His Kingdom, and once again cause His will to be done. They did not look for this to happen in some far distant future time or some far distant off-world place. They did not believe earth and heaven were far distant from one another: they believed that earth and heaven overlapped and interlocked with heaven as God's throne and earth as His footstool. They believed earth and heaven were most obviously joined in the

Temple. They did not believe that one day, when the Kingdom reached its final consummation, the earth would be abandoned in favor of some mysterious place called heaven.

So, when praying for the rise of the Kingdom, they were praying in anticipation. They believed God's Kingdom would rise, that God's will would be done throughout all the earth, and that the union of earth and heaven would be made manifest.

This prayer is driven by memory, present hope and faith concerning the future. The Jews celebrated those memories through their stories, their songs, and their feast days. They lived in submission to the present hope through obedience to Torah, and they anticipated the coming of the New and Final Exodus.

Sounds like more than just interesting history of an ancient people.

Very early in the ministry of Jesus, he presents Himself as the New Temple (see **John 2:19**), that place where earth and heaven are most surely joined. John said as much: **"The Word became flesh and made his dwelling among us. We have seen his glory, the glory of the One and Only, who came from the Father, full of grace and truth." (1:14)**. The teachings of Jesus present a new manner of living. His death conquers the tyrant that terrorized all of creation. His resurrection announces Him as the only rightful Lord with full authority in heaven and on earth.

In looking for the new Exodus, the Jews were looking for one who would cleanse/rebuild the Temple, establish a new way of life, conquer the oppressive tyrant, and rule as Lord of all.

Jesus satisfied all this and more, yet it looked nothing like what they expected. They missed the coming of the Kingdom.

Today, when we pray, **"your kingdom come, your will be done, on earth as it is in heaven,"** I trust we can pray with our eyes wide open.

We see in Jesus the coming of the Kingdom, the ever-present continuation of the Kingdom, and the promise of the final consummation of the Kingdom.

With the eyes of our understanding opened, let us pray this prayer in remembrance of Christ's work and in celebration of His Kingdom. The New Temple is now within those who belong to Christ; through the indwelling of the Spirit a holy manner of life is now possible, sin and death no longer have the ability to terrorize us, and Jesus is – right now, right here – the LORD OF ALL.

Let us tell the story. Let us sing the songs. Let us celebrate the feast of the Kingdom at the Lord's Table when we gather for worship.

As we pray this prayer, let us express our present hope through our obedience. Obedience is not simply an act of duty. Obedience is more than checking the boxes.

Obedience need not become a drudgery. Obedience is so much more than earning heaven and avoiding hell.

Obedience is an expression of present hope. We obey because we believe that Jesus is Lord, right here, right now. Our obedience is an expression of trust during the time of evil and suffering. Our obedience gives evidence of our trust in the final consummation of the Kingdom. Our present obedience declares, "Jesus Christ is Lord."

As we pray this prayer let us be alert to the working of the Kingdom all around us. We have adjusted our focus to see all the bad, ugly, disgusting, offensive, degrading, sinful, perverted, corrupt, fearful things of our world. Through such a focus we withdraw from the world, we despair for our children, we complain and criticize, we resign ourselves to the defeat of hope, and we long for a contra-biblical abandonment of this earth.

I am concerned that far too many of us are living in some form of dualism. We act as though darkness and Light are in a great battle with the outcome undetermined. We talk like the darkness is winning and our only option is to flee that darkness, to huddle in our safe sanctuaries, and to endure until the end. Whatever we say we believe our behavior sends this message: *the end better come soon before the darkness completely darks over.*

Now is the time for a transformation of our perspective. We must stop allowing the systems of this world to dictate what and how we see the world around us. Rather than fleeing from the darkness we must be the light. Now is the time to plead for the Father to give us eyes to see, ears to hear and hearts to perceive His Kingdom breaking out all around us. The Father will give us courage to run into the darkness with the Light.

We must stop the escapist longing for the final consummation of the Kingdom and start participating in the right-here, right-now, already work of the Kingdom.

Questions for reflection:

1. Describe the kingdom of this world –

2. How has this kingdom influenced our thinking about life?

3. How has this kingdom influenced our thinking about the Kingdom?

4. Describe the impact of an escapist mentality on how we live, how we interact with others, and how we care for creation.

5. Respond to this statement: "Obedience is an expression of present hope. We obey because we believe that Jesus is Lord, right here, right now."

25. DAILY BREAD

I certainly do not understand the issue of daily bread. Carol and I have two side-by-side refrigerator/freezer combos, a full-size freezer, a pantry, and numerous jars of canned produce hiding under the beds. Our struggle is not *if* we will eat: our struggle is to decide *what* we will eat from among our abundance.

Let's face it: most of us could eat for several days from our present stock of food without saying a single prayer about provision. And if we don't have what we want we can simply get in the car and go to the local restaurant.

Not so for the first audience. Their lives were a constant cycle of survival: gather seed, plant, cultivate, harvest, eat. Any breakdown in the cycle could mean destitution and starvation.

Even so, I do not believe they heard these words of Jesus – **"This, then, is how you should pray ...give us today our daily bread"** (vs. 11) – as simplistically as "I'm hungry, feed me."

This is not a prayer of indulgence: *just give me my food each day.*

From the earliest days God announced, **"by the sweat of your brow you will eat your food" (Genesis 3:19)**. Our efforts are part of the cycle of productivity by design and command. The Apostle Paul picks up on this truth:

> **"In the name of the Lord Jesus Christ, we command you, brothers, to keep away from every brother who is idle and does not live according to the teaching you received from us. For you yourselves know how you ought to follow our example. We were not idle when we were among you, nor did we eat anyone's food without paying for it. On the contrary, we worked night and day, laboring and toiling so that we would not be a burden to any of you. We did this, not because we do not have the right to such help, but in order to make ourselves a model for you to follow. For even when we were with you, we gave you this rule: 'If a man will not work, he shall not eat.'"** (2 Thessalonians 3:6-10)

This prayer for daily bread might first be heard as an implied call to work. If we should pray for bread, yet never use the abilities and opportunities provided us for productive labor, we would be hungry in the morning and go to bed with growling stomachs and God would remain just and good. Seeking the Father as the dispenser of bread and not the provider of strength is something we must carefully avoid.

---

[25] Edward Leigh Pell, *Our Troublesome Religious Questions,* (New York, Chicago, Toronto, London, Edinburgh: Fleming Revell Company, 1916), pg. 209.

"Jesus freely gave five thousand people their supper when they did not so much as ask for it; but when they began to seek him merely because they wanted more suppers, he would not give them a mouthful." [25]

There are times when we are without strength and must exist in a circumstance when our own hands cannot provide. The prophet Elijah experienced two such occasions. One is recorded in **1 Kings 17**. On that occasion God used birds to feed Elijah twice a day. The other occasion is recorded in **1 Kings 19.** Elijah had confronted the prophets of Baal on Mount Carmel. After that confrontation he fled for his life. While in hiding, an angel provided him with two meals of bread and water.

Many in that first audience immediately thought about the Great Exodus, that time when their ancestors were delivered from bondage by the mighty hand of God. Very soon after that deliverance God gave these words of promise to Moses: **"I will rain down bread from heaven for you. The people are to go out each day and gather enough for that day."** **(Exodus 16:4)**

What followed the promise was some forty years of miraculous provision which had to be gathered and prepared for eating.

Each sentence of this prayer stirred memories of the Exodus and longings for another great Exodus: God had done it before and He would do it again. This request for daily bread stirred both the memories and the longings. Could it be that this prayer for daily bread was a subtle promise of a soon to come Exodus? Is this teacher asking them to look through the lens of history to see the future? Is their God about to rise in deliverance and miraculous provision?

Jesus certainly has their direct attention. He has not just grabbed them by the ears: he has drawn them by the heart.

This prayer for daily bread is a call to remember past provision. A call to remember those times when God displayed his power and care. Those times when only a miracle would do and a miracle came.

As a young pastor in a less than lucrative assignment we faced need again and again. I needed work boots and had no ability to buy them. God provided. I needed tires on the car and had no ability to buy them. God provided. As our children grew out of their clothes and shoes, we could not go to the local retailer twice a year and buy them a new wardrobe. Yet time and time again someone would show up at our house with bags of clothes – the right kind of clothes in the needed sizes. Our refrigerator quit and was beyond repair. We had no choice but to live out of a picnic cooler. Then came the phone call that resulted in a brand-new side-by-side (which we still use some 25 years later). How that person found out about our need I will never know.

Even though I am not experiencing such neediness right now, I still remember. God provided what was needed when it was needed. Again and again. And I remember.

Those memories fuel my faith whenever I face a need today. The Father who took care of me then will take care of me now.

This prayer for daily bread is a call to trust, to live in dependence, to recognize God as the ultimate Provider. It is the Father who provides the sun, the rain, seedtime and harvest in fulfillment of His promise: **"As long as the earth endures, seedtime and harvest, cold and heat, summer and winter, day and night will never cease" (Genesis 8:22)**. It is the Father who gives understanding each day so that we can perform the tasks of our employment. It is the Father who gives strength so that we can earn that payday. It is through the gracious manipulations of the Father that we encounter opportunities for work so that we can live in the integrity of our bills being paid.

Today is a day when the Father is at work so that we, too, might be at work.

This prayer for daily bread is a call to look into the future with faith. The Father who provided yesterday, the Father who is providing today, is the Father who will provide tomorrow. He was faithful yesterday, He is faithful today, and He will be faithful tomorrow. This does not mean tomorrow's bread will taste like yesterday's bread. It does not mean that today's bread will provide us with left-overs for tomorrow. The Father will do each day that which expresses his will, brings him glory and provides our need. The taste of today need not dictate our trust for tomorrow.

We must remember what the Father has done; we must recognize what the Father is doing; we must trust in what the Father will do. This is part of praying, "**give us today our daily bread.**"

We should be telling the stories, singing the songs, and celebrating the unwavering faithfulness of God. God has been, is and will continue to be faithful!

This prayer for daily bread is a call to live in right-now relationship with the Father. This relationship is marked by His provision and our submission; He graciously gives, we gratefully receive. As children of this faithful Father we have less reason to complain than anyone. In this right-now relationship we are learning to measure the Father's provision not by *how much* but by *how faithful.* Once we learn this lesson we no longer complain that the Father has not provided enough. Rather, we will rejoice in gratitude for his faithfulness.

This prayer for daily bread is a call to contentment in simplicity. Jesus did not say "give us today our daily steak and eggs." Contrary to the focus on prosperity found in many American churches, it appears Jesus calls us to contentment in simplicity. He peels away the veneer of materialism and gets to the heart of the matter. Can we embrace those memories of simple provision as good memories? Can we receive today's simple provision with gratitude? Can we look into a future marked by simple provisions with a peaceful heart?

Contentment in simplicity is what will enable us to bow our heads in equal gratitude for dry toast and water as for a grand buffet.

Memory. Dependence. Trust. Relationship. Contentment.

These are the real ingredients of this daily bread.

Questions for reflection:

1. How does our culture influence our dissatisfaction?

2. How has the church embraced this cultural dissatisfaction?

3. Respond to this statement: "This prayer for daily bread might first be heard as an implied call to work."

4. Recall a time when God provided for you or your family, either in a direct way or through making work available.

5. How did that moment of provision impact you?

26. RELEASE FROM DEBT

In the life cycle of the Jewish people, every 50th year was to be a year of Jubilee: **"Consecrate the fiftieth year and proclaim liberty throughout the land to all its inhabitants."** (**Leviticus 25:10**)

During the celebrations of the year of Jubilee, all land was to be returned to the original owner, all debts were to be forgiven, and all slaves set free.

Can you imagine the anticipation of the Jubilee? Can you hear the voice of the old patriarch as he reminds the family, again, that in just a few months they will return to their family home? Can you hear the father explain to the family gathered for a meal that in a little over a year their crushing debt will be erased? Can you hear the excited whispers of slaves huddled over a small fire as they talk of what they will do once they are set free?

The national atmosphere must have crackled with the anticipation of Jubilee. There was no other celebration like it in the life cycle of the people of Israel. It was not just a red-letter day on the calendar: it was a **CAPITAL RED LETTER** year.

It was the time when God reminded his people that both the land and the people belong to him (see **Leviticus 25:23,55**). It was the year when God brought the covenant relationship into visible, tangible form. Restoration, release, freedom, trust were realities of the covenant. In the Jubilee those things were practiced and experienced as more than a fanciful theory.

When Jesus said, **"This, then, is how you should pray: forgive us our debts as we also have forgiven our debtors"** (vs.12) that first audience immediately heard the subtle tones of Jubilee. Their minds remembered stories of land restored, debts forgiven, and slaves set free.

They heard a call for release and restoration. Jesus called them to recognize their need for release and restoration and their obligation to release and restore others. God purchased Israel with a strong hand and delivered them from slavery to establish a theocratic society. They could never repay God for these miraculous works. Can you imagine what would have happened if God had called the nation to an accounting? If God called Moses and the tribal leaders up on the mountain and handed them a ledger and began a discussion about repayment? Israel was indebted beyond any possibility of repayment. I can hear how God might bring this discussion to its conclusion: "Here is how this is going to work: from this day forward, you are mine. The people, all the resources, all the land – everyone and everything – are mine. I will be your God; you will be my people. We will live in covenantal relationship. In that relationship you will find a freedom far beyond anything provided by a repayment plan. Your freedom will be found in this covenantal relationship. Here are the details..."

Today, in this prayer, we hear a call to restoration and release.

1 Corinthians 6:19-20 – "You are not your own; you were bought at a price." The same God who worked in such mighty and miraculous ways to deliver and establish Israel, has also worked in mighty and miraculous ways on our behalf. Can you imagine what it would be like if God suddenly called us into an accounting? If he handed us a ledger and began a discussion of a repayment plan? Jesus brought such questions into focus in **Matthew 18.** A servant with an impossible debt was called to give an account. That debt was equal to 150,000 years wages. (That would mean that if I earn $40,000 a year I would be in debt *$6 billion dollars.*) The only hope for that servant was the absorbing and releasing forgiveness of the master. The master would absorb the debt and release the servant. In this parable Jesus dramatically illustrates our indebtedness to the Father. Our only hope is in the absorbing and releasing grace of the Father, grace provided by the Son and applied by the Spirit.

This absorbing and releasing grace is not exclusively applied in one trip to an altar.

Living broken lives in a fallen world creates a continual flow of indebtedness. We will never live at a level of personal holiness that puts us at sum zero. There will never come a time when we attain such spiritual brilliance that we are no longer indebted to the Father. We will always owe more than we have any hope of repaying.

That is why Jesus taught us to pray **"forgive us our debts"**. Through the flow of absorbing and releasing grace you and I live as free in a covenantal relationship with God the Father.

Hallelujah!

Jesus went on to inform us that we are under obligation to do as the Father is doing: give absorbing and releasing grace to others – **"...as we have forgiven our debtors."**

We are not good at giving absorbing and releasing grace. Not good at it at all.

We are much better at creating indebtedness, keeping a record of indebtedness, and making efforts to collect indebtedness.

"How do we do that?" you ask.

How often have we said something like: "I did a good deed for that person and I have yet to receive any kind of 'thank you.' We'll see if I do another good thing for them."

With those words we express a heart attitude that creates debt, records debt, with a desire to collect debt. If the debt is not satisfied we experience a relational bankruptcy.

All in contrast to the implications of this prayer.

How about this: "That person really did me wrong and they owe me an apology"? Does that phrase, or the thousands of variations it can take, sound familiar?

Once again, we express a heart attitude that creates debt, records debt, with a desire to collect debt. And again, if the debt is not satisfied we experience a relational bankruptcy.

"I was really disappointed, let down, or offended. That person owes me an explanation."

Yep, we've done it again.

Right now, most of us are remembering such an event. If you are the debt holder, may I offer a firm grace suggestion? *Release that person and that debt.* Make the call. Write the letter. Arrange the appointment.

Some individuals will hold to these debts for decades. They will hold to them even after the debt is paid. "You know, it took that person ten months to say 'thank you.'" "That person did not apologize for six years."

How quickly we forget the principle of love given in **1 Corinthians 13:5 "It** [love] **keeps no record of wrongs."**

God demands we do as he is continually doing: offer absorbing and releasing grace.

Contrary to the Biblical principles of forgiveness, offering forgiveness to others is not the way we are set free. True forgiveness, modeled after the forgiveness God provided and for which we are asking in this prayer, absorbs the debt and releases the debtor. You and I did not pay our way into a forgiven status: God through Christ absorbed all the cost necessary so that we could be given the free gift of forgiveness. We must come to the place where we never say, "I'll forgive that person *when they...*" By the maturing work of the Spirit through prayer, we must come to the place where we have a continual flow of forgiveness toward any and all who wrong us. Our immediate response is absorbing and releasing forgiveness. We take the pain, the hurt, the damage; we release the debt and erase the record. We will no longer hold that individual accountable to our pain, disappointment, or offense. They are free and owe us nothing.

Just let it go! Stop telling and retelling the story. Throw away the record. Then accept the absorbing and releasing grace of the Father that will cleanse our carnal and rebellious heart.

Isn't that how the free gift of forgiveness from God works in our life? And aren't we to pattern our forgiveness after His?

Romans 13:8 helps us understand there is only one legitimate debt we owe one another. This is the continuing debt to love one another. This debt supersedes all others. This debt effectively cancels all others.

The practice of absorbing, releasing forgiveness causes our fellowship gatherings to become a safe place. No more gossip. No more holding a grudge. No more double standard: asking for God's gracious forgiveness while offering conditional forgiveness to others. Our gatherings become a place where the words of **James** are reality: **"Confess your sins to each other and pray for each other so that you may be healed"** (5:16).

> "In confession there takes place a *breakthrough to community.* Sin wants to be alone with people. It takes them away from community. Sin wants to remain unknown. It shuns the light. In confession the light of the gospel breaks into the darkness and closed isolation of the heart. Sin that has been spoken and confessed has lost all of its power. We can admit our sins and in this very act find community for the first time. Only another Christian who is under the cross can hear my confession. It is not experience with life but experience with the cross that makes one suited to hear confession." [26]

If we do not purposefully and intentionally participate in the flow of absorbing and releasing grace we will live in the poverty of spiritual secrecy.

Spiritual poverty is not the Father's plan for us. He wants us to live to the full. To live in daily Jubilee. To be released and restored and to offer release and restoration.

---

[26] Dietrich Bonhoeffer, *Life Together Prayerbook of the Bible,* General Editor Wayne Whitson Floyd, Jr., (Minneapolis: Fortress Press, 2005), pgs. 110, 115.

To enjoy the holy celebration of freedom that comes from receiving and giving absorbing and releasing grace.

Questions for reflection:

1) How does our culture view the idea of forgiveness?

2) What indebtedness might you be carrying right now?

3) What indebtedness are you enforcing upon the life of another person?

4) What stories are your default stories of wrongs done to you?

5) Is there a trusted, maturing Christian who would be willing to hear your confession? If so, when will you make such an appointment?

27. DELIVERANCE

"This, then, is how you should pray...lead us not into temptation, but deliver us from the evil one." (vs. 13)

I have struggled on how to approach and present this portion of the prayer. Both **James - "Consider it pure joy, my brothers, whenever you face trials of many kinds, ..."** (1:2) and **Peter – "These have come so that your faith...may be proved genuine..."** (1 Pet. 1:7) deal with the issue of trials and testing in a somewhat positive light.

The Bible does not encourage the seeking of trials or tests, but it does assure us that God is at work through the trials for a grand purpose. We are encouraged to endure and trust the faithfulness of God to bring forth his purpose in those times.

Jesus seems to be encouraging us – actually instructing us to make it a matter of prayer – to ask the Father to cause our life to avoid those times of testing and trial (for those of you who think I am simply confused, the word *temptation* in **Matthew 6:13** is the same word used by **James** and by **Peter**).

If God works in and through trials and testing for his purpose and our good why would we ask to be led another way?

Context clears this up a bit. Both **James** and **Peter** put these trials and tests in a life context of spiritual growth and maturity: the work of holiness is advanced beyond theory into practical reality by these times of test and trial. Jesus puts them in the context of an encounter with the evil one. When seen in such a context, Jesus was consistent in admonishing his disciples to pray for avoidance (see: **Matthew 26:41; Mark 14:38; Luke 22:40, 46**).

This prayer is pleading with the Father that he not lead us into an encounter with the evil one.

Being led by God was not a new concept among God's people. Those in that first audience could recite how God led Abraham, Isaac, Jacob, Joseph, Moses, and Joshua. They could tell of the miraculous leading God provided for them as a people. They could quote the Psalms inspired by the theme of God leading his people.

They understood this idea of leading as God's way of carrying, or bringing, his people to a place he desired them to be. The path might be a difficult one but it never led to an overwhelming encounter with the Evil One. They knew that God never leads his people into a place or time of spiritual failure; he always leads them into a place and time of increasing relational holiness.

They see this prayer as one of both confession and submission.

As should we.

We must confess that we do not have the wisdom to choose our own path. The Bible warns of our folly in such an effort: **"There is a way that seems right to a man but in the end it leads to death." (Proverbs 16:25)**

Left to my own wisdom I will not always choose the worst path, but neither will I be capable of always choosing the best path. I will consistently choose that which is short-sighted and selfishly satisfying. I am not equipped to see what good might come from a path of difficulty or what weakness might come from a path of ease.

Our fallen nature will choose the path which leads toward less personal responsibility, less personal accountability, and more toward some ill-defined freedom. The paths that we most often choose are not paths toward increasing relational holiness with the Father or our faith family.

The path we choose leads to a small world. A world of population *me* and anyone who affirms me, accepts me without challenge, and supports me just as I am.

If our lives are to progress successfully, our path must be dictated by the Father. If our lives are going to grow they must be led into the provisions of the **"green pastures"** and the restoration of the **"still waters."**

God has placed appropriate desires in all of us. Basic among those desires are the desire for intimacy, the desire for significance, and a desire to influence. These desires can, and often do, cause us to establish certain behavioral patterns. If we allow our desire for intimacy to be joined to the systems of this world we will be led into patterns of sinful behavior and illegitimate sexuality. If we allow our desire for significance to be joined with the systems of this world we will be led into increasing self-centeredness. When our desire for influence is handled in this way we will be enticed by the corruption of power. The Scripture found in **James** states it this way: **"Each one is tempted when he is drawn away by his own desires and enticed."** (**1:14** NKJV)

When I choose my own path it will inevitable lead me to encounters with that which entices me to sin. My web searches will take me "this close." My entertainment choices will invite me to linger near the enticements. Even my route through the retail store will take me past that which allures me.

And when I get "that close", when I linger near, when I walk in sight-line of temptation, I will be enticed. In that moment my lack of wisdom exposes a lack of strength and sin in born.

Consider the words of my friend, John Lawson:

> "Temptation is not a sin. There, I said it. However, don't stop reading here. You would give me a great big thumbs up if I just stopped here. After all, we enjoy our flirtatious relationship with temptation. To some, temptation might mean to sip, rather than to chug. It might mean to look, but to not touch. It may mean to gamble for quarters, rather than dollars.

Temptation is not a sin, but entertaining temptation can become a sin."
(johnalawson.wordpress.com/2018/01/09)

We need the Father to set our path.

The Father's path allows us to take our desire for intimacy and find ways for that to be expressed in deepening relational holiness. The Father's path allows our desire for significance to be expressed in sacrificial service. The Father's path allows our desire for influence to be expressed as being his witness.

Since I lack the necessary wisdom and strength, I am required to make at least one more confession: I am not equipped for a one-on-one confrontation with the evil one.

I remember listening to a college ministerial student preaching in student chapel many years ago. He was leaving no room for misunderstanding: he hated the devil. To add emphasis to his words, he left the platform, walked front and center, and unleashed a mighty kick at the devil.

He fell and a mighty fall it was.

The man who says he wants an encounter with the devil so he can punch him in the face, kick him in the seat, or "spit 'baccer juice in his eye" is deluded.

Those who believe they can approach the devil, step on his neck, and show they have dominion over him are deluded.

The devil is a powerful foe. His accusations are overwhelming. His deceptions are superbly disguised. His light is a near-perfect counterfeit. In ourselves we are no match for him. Human history is an undeniable testimony to the successes of his methods.

Even so, he is not the equal opposite of Christ. Christ handed the devil the ultimate defeat on the Cross and through the empty tomb. It is through the victory of Christ that we are victorious. We are told to resist the devil (**1 Peter 5:9**) and after putting on the armor of God to simply stand (**Ephesians 6:13**). We stand upon the victory of Christ, a sure and certain place to stand.

These confessions lead me to a statement of submission: I must submit to the leading of the Father.

I do not have the wisdom. I do not have the strength. I do not have the skills or the tools.

I must submit to the leading of the Father and trust the path he chooses for me. I must trust in his gracious guidance. He never takes me into something He cannot take me through.

The Father's name will be known as holy along the path he chooses for me.

The Father's kingdom will come and his will be done as I submit to the path he chooses.

The Father's daily provisions will be known as I walk the path he chooses.

The Father's forgiveness will be known and the ability to forgive will be learned as I make the journey along the path he chooses.

This is a good path, even if it is a difficult one.

This path is a sanctified path, even if it is not always a safe one.

This path is a certain path, even when it is not clearly seen.

This path is not simply the means to a grand destination. This path is the very beginnings of that grand destination.

Questions for reflection:

1) How does our culture view the idea of temptation?   The Devil?

2) In what ways has the church been less than transparent about the issue of temptation?

3) What temptation is most effective in luring you?

4) What methods in responding to that temptation have you tried? Failure or success?

5) How will this portion of the Lord's Prayer impact your resistance to temptation?

28. FORGIVE

A college student wrote his dad and asked for money. Several days later the young man received a return letter from his dad. Anticipating money, the young man ripped open the envelope and began to read. It was a nice letter, filled with details from home. And then it had this post script: "I would have enclosed $20 but I already sealed the envelope."

Many of us understand the idea behind the *post script*, or PS. One more important detail needs to be added, one more reminder, one more bit of information, one more romantic phrase.

Jesus finished presenting how to pray. The model prayer he presented is powerful and convicting. If that model is used as our example, we will come to better understand the subtle nuances of communication with the Father. Beyond rote memorization, learning to hear the words of Jesus - **"This, then, is how you should pray"** - is a life-long class in which there is advancement but from which there is no graduation.

Jesus now adds a PS: **"For if you forgive men when they sin against you, your heavenly Father will also forgive you. But if you do not forgive men their sins, your Father will not forgive your sins."** (vss. 14-15)

Most people add a "PS" to their ideas about prayer. The ancient Jews added to prayer the particulars about hand position and movement, about body position and movement, about how to enter the place of prayer and how to exit the place of prayer. It was as though they would say, "Pray like this and don't forget to_____." These PS expressions are not meant to replace prayer neither do they enhance the power of prayer. These PS expressions discipline the entire person into the recognition of the uniqueness and holiness of prayer. They remind us of the carefulness that should influence our approach to the God of heaven.

We attach our own forms of PS. Fold your hands, close your eyes, pray aloud, use King James English, use a different kind of voice, speak in tongues – the list is long. We say, "Pray, and don't forget to _____." We know these things do not replace prayer or enhance the power of prayer. These PS expressions are how we discipline ourselves as we approach the God of heaven.

Jesus said, **"This, then, is how you should pray...and forgive...forgive...forgive..."**

Forgiveness.

I see Matthew as he remembers this occasion. I see him pause, deep in thought, recalling the wording Jesus used. The word he remembers Jesus using when speaking of forgiveness is a strong and powerful word. It had been used for centuries to describe the act of sending away, hurling away, releasing, letting go, leaving behind, abandoning, dismissing, or setting aside. It was a word used to describe a decisive, purposeful, intentional and final act.

The act of forgiving is to be a decisive act, filled with purpose and finality.

An act completely contrary to our nature.

We love to tell of how God forgave our sins. We love to tell about people we know who experienced deep and transforming forgiveness through Christ. We love to declare that God is ready to forgive any and all who will confess and repent. We are blessed by the knowledge that once forgiven, those sins are gone. They are really *gone.* God, by an act of Divine power, forgets them: it is now impossible for those sins to ever re-enter the record of our life. Have you ever meditated upon this glorious truth? We celebrate a God of such absurd love and indescribable grace.

And we love to tell how we will forgive others but cannot forget. We are not referring to the bio-chemical impossibility of forgetting: we mean we cannot – *will not* – forget what was done to us. "Fool me once, shame on you; fool me twice, shame on me." We just won't forget. How could we? We keep the memories fresh by telling the story of our injury over, and over, and over...*ad nauseam.* We never give grace the opportunity to fade not only the scars but also the story.

Pastors are among the most consistent offenders in this regard. I know this: I am a pastor and I have been grossly guilty. A hurt received, forgiveness given, and now a story to tell. We justify ourselves by declaring, "I have to vent and get this off my chest." And we do - every time there is any kind of pastors' gathering. I tell my story of injury. And then another pastor tells a more dramatic story. And then another. It quickly becomes a carnal display of one-upmanship. One day the Lord spoke right into my heart: *"Your retelling of this story is a disguised form of unforgiveness. Stop it. Now."* Each time one of those old stories begs to be told yet again (and 30+ years of pastoral ministry provide plenty of such stories) I hear that Voice: *"Stop. Now."*

Our nature wants to grab, hold and nurse our injuries. We want to tell the story, to vent, again and again. It reminds us that we are the victim. It forces our closest friends to pick a side – our side – and sympathize with us.

We want the person who wronged us to know how badly they hurt us. We want them to be held accountable, we want them to pay, we want justice (most often this justice is simply a poorly disguised pursuit of vengeance), and we want our pound of flesh.

Families are split and friendships severed all because someone wants to hold on to some offense, nurse some wound, continually recall some hurt.

Churches are debilitated when someone refuses to forgive, refuses to let go, refuses to stop telling the story. Gossip is a wicked and godless activity. Gossip will not yield to love, which does no harm to others. Gossip will not yield to truth. Gossip rejects the presence of the Savior. Where gossip exists unchallenged, the glory of God has departed. Gossip is one of the most damaging and damning expressions of an unforgiving spirit in the world of the church.

Have you even been on a board or committee when a secretary had to be selected from among the group? Most of us find all manner of reasons why we are decidedly not qualified for the task. Memory's no good. Not good with words. Terrible grammar. Taking notes would just be a distraction. Might miss a meeting or two. Our life affirms these excuses. We can't remember what to pick up at the grocery store. We forget to return email and text messages. We overlook the mundane.

All this is true until we have been wronged.

We can recount the offense in vivid detail. We remember names, dates, locations, body language, facial expressions, words that were said and amazingly we even remember words that were not said. This vivid recall can be triggered in an instant. We never say, "It seems like something happened but I can't remember the details."

We struggle to handle these expressions of an unforgiving spirit.

One pastor friend told me the story of a person in the church who stated: "I cannot, I will not, forgive that person. They hurt me so badly." This person would make such an announcement in small groups and to anyone who would hear the tale of woe. The pastor was understandably stressed by this situation. My advice went something like this: "You need to schedule a time for a moment of firm-grace confrontation. From the Scriptures help them understand our obligation to forgive any and all who wrong us. Leave them nowhere to go but to their knees. If they refuse to hear your counsel, as pastor you have the authority to begin an appropriate disciplinary process. This must not be allowed to go unchallenged."

Two Biblical truths are often neglected when facing the challenge of forgiving others.

One of those is found in **Matthew 18:15-19:**

> **"If your brother sins against you, go and show him his fault, just between the two of you. If he listens to you, you have won your bother over. But if he will not listen, take one or two others along, so that every matter may be established by the testimony of two or three witnesses. If he refuses to listen to them, tell it to the church; and if he refuses listen even to the church, treat him as you would a pagan or tax collector. I tell you the truth, whatever you bind on earth will be bound in heaven, and whatever you loose on earth will be loosed in heaven. Again, I tell you that if two of you on earth agree about anything you ask for, it will be done for**

you by my Father in heaven. For where two or three come together in my name, there am I with them."

There will be a time when a fellow Christian will sin against you, or you against them. Jesus outlined, in very clear detail, how such an event is to be handled. The very power and authority of heaven rests upon such action. According to Jesus, this process of reconciliation has two conditional promises: the promise of the Father's involvement and supply and the presence of Christ himself.

In our fear of this process, we choose to hold a grudge, spread gossip, present overly-detailed prayer requests (a poorly disguised form of gossip), and walk in the darkness of unforgiven sin.

How in the world did we ever come to believe our way is less fearful, less painful, less damaging?

Help us Jesus!

The second Biblical truth is found in **Matthew 18:21-35.** You know the story. A servant is called to give an account for an impossible debt. The master chooses to forgive the debt and let the servant go. That servant went out and abused a fellow servant over a manageable debt. That ungrateful servant was then imprisoned by the master until he could pay all he owed. Then these words: **"This is how my heavenly Father will treat each of you unless you forgive your brother from your heart"** (vs. 35).

This story gives us a few principles about forgiveness: 1) in forgiving another, we are not finding freedom for ourselves, but for them. We choose to let them go; 2) in forgiving another, the debt does not simply vanish: we embrace the debt, we take on the burden, and release the offender; 3) once forgiven, we are under Divine obligation to offer the same as we have been given: absorbing, releasing grace. True forgiveness is not based on a selfish motivation; it is an act of sacrificial humility.

In this post script to prayer, Jesus gives this hard reality to those in his Kingdom: forgiveness must be active to be received. We cannot hold unforgiveness, however we choose define it, and expect the forgiving grace of the heavenly Father to remain currently active in our own life. We all need to live in the fresh flow of the Father's forgiveness. There will be moments when our words, actions, attitude, or thought patterns will be contrary to God's intention. In those moments we will need forgiveness. Each time. Every time.

We cannot live with an unforgiving spirit toward others and live in the necessary flow of the Father's forgiveness. We will not receive what we refuse to give.

We must forgive others. We must let it go. We must leave it behind. We must abandon the story. We must dismiss the record. We must tear the pages out of our life journal. We must take decisive, purposeful, intentional action with a sense of finality.

A few years ago, my wife and I experienced a terrible injustice. The pain was deep. From that pain arose a quiet, seething anger. I made several entries in my personal journal giving expression to my struggle. A few months ago, the Lord prompted me to remove those pages from my journal. Removing those pages was a deeply symbolic moment: forgiveness took on a deeper reality as I truly let go of that event.

If we refuse to take such action something powerful happens: the wrong done to us becomes the wrong that is now in us.

This begs a question, does it not?

Could the presence of unforgiveness toward others, and the consequential lack of current forgiveness for ourselves, be that which is causing so many issues and dysfunctions in both the life of believers and in the church?

I believe a great, sweeping flood of the presence and power of God will be known among us the moment we allow the convicting and cleansing grace of Christ to wash away our spirit of unforgiveness.

Questions for reflection:

1) How does our culture handle the idea of forgiving others?

2) How has this cultural idea influenced the church?

3) How has this cultural idea influenced you?

4) What choice of forgiveness do you need to make right now?

29. FASTING

Fasting has been a part of the national and personal practice among the Jews since their earliest history. In times of crisis, impending danger, or in a time of disaster, a fast was proclaimed. This proclamation was made by the king or by a prophet and was a time of repentance, the renewal of covenant, and marked by a reversal of conduct.

An individual could volunteer to fast in response to personal distress, danger, or as part of repentance.

Fasting was not permitted on the Sabbath except during Yom Kippur. Fasting was always considered a time to afflict the soul and the Sabbath was a day of delight in God: the two were not considered compatible.

The first century Jew still practiced fasting; when Jesus spoke of the practice of fasting this first audience understood his meaning.

> **"When you fast, do not look somber as the hypocrites do, for they disfigure their face to show men they are fasting. I tell you the truth, they have received their reward in full. But when you fast, put oil on your head and wash your face, so that it will not be obvious to men that you are fasting, but only to your Father, who is unseen; and your Father, who**

sees what is done in secret, will reward you." (vss. 16-18)

Fasting, along with the other two spiritual practices highlighted in the teachings of Jesus (giving and prayer, 6:2ff, 6:5ff), needs careful attention. If our real enemy cannot keep us from these significant practices then he will tempt us to pervert them through self-righteousness.

Jesus identifies this hypocrisy: any time the spiritual practice is joined with publicity or driven by self-centered motives, that is hypocrisy.

Hypocrites give to be seen and applauded by others.

Hypocrites pray to be heard and applauded by others.

Hypocrites fast to build reputation among others.

In each case, what was meant to be a deeply personal and intensely significant spiritual practice, becomes another manifestation of sinful flesh.

Hypocrisy receives its full reward right here, right now. The empty, fleeting, powerless, unholy applause of men is the full reward. Nothing more. Nothing else. Only the sound of mortal flesh being pounded together.

Jesus counsels us to consider fasting, and the other spiritual practices of giving and prayer, like a confidentiality agreement between us and the Father.

An Audience of the One.

Nothing more. Nothing else. Just the attention of the Eternal God who is Holy, Holy, Holy.

We are urged to continue our usual routines when we are fasting. We must not look miserable in an effort to bait people into asking if we're okay so we can tell them about our fasting. We must not do anything or appear in any way out of the ordinary to prompt questions that would give us a chance to whisper our righteousness.

We must disguise our spiritual practices so thoroughly that they are obvious only to the Father.

When it comes to fasting, there is no supernatural power in simply not eating.

That would just be weird.

Fasting has several layers. Elmer Towns, in his book *Know God Through Fasting,* offers the following layers:

Emptying. The emptying of ourselves of food is meant to symbolize our emptying of self. God cannot fill someone who is already full of themselves. Self is an insidious presence in the secret place of the heart. Fasting puts in practice the words of **Psalm 139:23-24: "Search me, O God, and know my heart; test me and know my anxious thoughts. See if there is any offensive way in me, and lead me in the way everlasting."**

Tasting. Not of food, but a much deeper tasting of the goodness of the Lord. This tasting is the rediscovery that Christ and Christ alone truly satisfies. We feast upon the richness of the Word and marinate in the presence of the Father of love. The Scripture becomes reality: **"Taste and see that the LORD is good; blessed is the man who takes refuge in him." (Psalm 34:8)**

Waiting. In a world where everything moves with blazing speed, waiting is a lost concept. Fasting slows our world to a moment of stillness, a moment when we can hear, **"Be still and know that I am God; I will be exalted among the nations, I will be exalted in the earth." (Psalm 46:10)** In the stillness of waiting we are reminded the Giver is greater than the gifts; waiting on Him is far better than expecting from Him.

Coming. Fasting is a clear declaration we intend to come into the presence of the Father. We are responding to His invitation. We are being drawn by His presence. We are coming. We are leaving the table and its bounty so that we might feast upon the presence of Christ. We are turning a deaf ear to the appetites of the body so we might indulge the appetites of the soul.

Fasting is often used, and even promoted, as a tool whereby we might manipulate God. We pray and pray and no answer or change of circumstance is apparent. We say, "I can't seem to get God to answer my prayer. I guess I will pray and fast."

We act as though God simply cannot resist a request made by prayer and fasting.

Some treat fasting like some hurry-up method to spiritual greatness. We can delude ourselves into believing that fasting is some kind of short-cut; through fasting we can arrive at a spiritual place without all the work and waiting.

These attitudes miss the point and are in contrast with the very spirit of fasting.

Fasting is not about me discovering a method to get my way.

Fasting is about me becoming intentional in allowing God to have His way.

Fasting is a secret interchange between me and the Father. I pour out so that He may pour in. I empty so He might fill. I seek Him so that I might be more fully found by Him.

Jesus says there is a divine reward waiting for those who will practice secret fasting. That certainly perks up our ears: tell us more! We love the idea of rewards. We choose credit cards based on cash back rewards. We enroll in a bank account that offers points that can be exchanged for rewards. We request a perks card from retailers we prefer. We are surrounded by those alluring messages of rewards.

If we are not careful we will lump fasting in among the other perks cards. If I do *this* it will give me *that*.

I don't see Jesus meaning such a thing when he speaks of the reward of the Father to those who practice fasting.

What if the reward is *not* God finally being forced to concede to our requests?

What if the reward is *not* finally being filled with enough power to do something supernatural?

What if the reward is *not* some launching pad into spiritual grandeur?

What if the reward is *not* any *thing*?

What if the reward is *not* some kind of super tool?

What if the reward is God Himself?

"At the end...you want to stay on the fast. You have been enjoying the presence of God, and you don't want to leave. You don't want to go back to the world of food..." [27]

---

[27] Elmer Towns, *Knowing God Through Fasting,* (Shippensburg, PA: Destiny Image Publishers, Inc., 2002), pg. 25,26.

Questions for reflection:

1) In a culture that thrives on applause, how does this teaching of Jesus find acceptance?

2) How does the idea of 'silent sacrifice' fit the culture of the American church?

3) What is your greatest personal challenge to fasting?

4) Respond to this statement: *"What if the reward is God Himself?"*

30. TREASURE

Our love of accumulation is so strong in our nature that we must be on constant guard.

Consider these statements about treasure: "We gather what we treasure." "We protect what we treasure." "Our thoughts are never far from our treasure." "Our motives are shaped by that which we treasure." "We mourn the loss of treasure."

Consider what Jesus says about treasure:

> **"Do not store up for yourselves treasures on earth, where moth and rust destroy, and where thieves break in and steal. But store up for yourselves treasures in heaven, where moth and rust do not destroy, and where thieves do not break in and steal. For where your treasure is, there your heart will be also. The eye is the lamp of the body. If your eyes are good, your whole body will be full of light. But if your eyes are bad, you whole body will be full of darkness. If then the light within you is darkness, how great is that darkness! No one can serve two masters. Either he will hate the one and love the other, or he will be devoted to the one and despise the other. You cannot serve both God and money."** (vss. 19-24).

Very few will admit, "I am a person who really struggles with serving money rather than serving God."

Most of us are more likely to say, "I am not a wealthy person so I do not have the means to buy all these supposed treasures. I can only maintain life necessities."

Through years of ministry, and personal experience, I have discovered selfishness, grasping, and hoarding are not issues generated by financial circumstances.

Treasures are not really a money issue. Treasures are a heart issue or an eye issue as we will discuss in a moment.

Jesus presents this warning about treasures because He knows treasures have the ability to steal away our hearts, our time, our money, and our relationships. When earthly things take on the status of treasures we are allowing the temporary to dictate the eternal and we are selling righteousness for the price of a trinket.

The issue of treasures has several red flags, warning signs meant to alert us to danger. Consider these warning signs:

We refuse to throw anything away...

Our financial records show we are more willing to finance an exotic personal vacation than to give generously to mission efforts...

Our expenditures show we will more quickly finance a clothing allowance than provide crisis care kits for those experiencing disaster...

We are more willing to spend substantial money to eat out than to give to those who provide food for the hungry...

We make sure we can afford a nice car at the expense of our ability to support the local church...

Our Christmas budget is more than our annual giving to the work of the Lord...

Yes, I hear you, "Hey, mind your own business!" You're right, your finances are not my business.

But the Lord made them His business.

And He instructed us to *not* store up treasures on earth, but to **"store up treasures in heaven."**

When we behave as citizens of Christ's Kingdom, we will use the things we treasure for heavenly good. We allow the eternal to dictate the earthly. We choose to give rather than to gather. We purposefully redirect our resources into that which matters most.

Jesus takes a left turn in the conversation without the benefit of a turn signal. He interrupts the talk about treasures with talk about our eyes. This interruption seems dramatically out of place.

Unless we take the time to understand.

Could it be Jesus is telling us that how we see things has a direct effect upon how we value those things?

If we see our abilities, our opportunities, and our resources as things to be used to further the Kingdom of Christ, to promote the Light and the Good News, then our **"eyes are good."** This way of seeing fills our life with light. This light gives life, dispels darkness, provides fellowship, and marks the right path. This way of seeing cannot, will not, be compartmentalized. It cannot be restricted to spiritual or church things. Jesus said this way of seeing fills the whole body with light. Family, school, work, social media, relationships, money, time, use of words...the *whole* of who we are will be filled with light when we see in this way.

If we see our abilities, our opportunities, and our resources as tools by which we can indulge our own interests, advance our own agenda, and increase our own accumulation, then our eyes are bad. We attempt to disguise our bad eyes by testifying to the blessings of God: "Oh, God has blessed me with a new car." "God has blessed us with a great vacation." "God has blessed me with a promotion." And yet our life record shows we use these blessings for personal indulging. We prove by our choices that how we see life is tainted by selfishness. And such seeing fills us with darkness. This darkness will not be contained or compartmentalized. It is a total darkness, affecting the whole of life. This darkness blinds us. This darkness causes us to lose our way. This darkness disorients and confuses us. This darkness breeds fear. This is a darkness that reproduces itself, even while denying its own existence. This darkness hides our sins, even from our own seeing.

Jesus declared it a great darkness. To take that which is meant to be light and use it for selfish indulgence – to take that meant for light and use it for darkness – creates a deep, intense, great darkness. A darkness from which there is no escape except through the transforming power of grace.

By now someone is raising this explanation (which is just a cleverly worded objection): "Well, I believe that after giving my tithe what I do with the rest of my money is up to me."

Jesus smiles and says, "Not so! **You cannot serve two masters.**"

You cannot serve God with some percentage and serve self with the rest.

Serving is a matter of the heart. We cannot set our heart on earthly things and serve a heavenly Master. We cannot set our heart on selfish indulgence and serve a Giving Lord. We cannot set our heart on stuff and serve the Savior.

Not possible.

A divided heart invites the worst kind of turmoil. A turmoil that will force a choice.

The danger of a divided heart is that it always leads to choosing self. A divided heart always serves self before serving the Savior.

If we hear these words of Jesus, if we keep our heart undivided and our vision clear – *we will have a single view of life*: recognizing who we are and what we have are meant for the Master's use.

We must have a single Master for life: Christ and Christ alone.

We are faced with one simple question. An incredibly difficult yet simple question:

> *Am I fully surrendered to the Lordship of Christ?*

For two millennia the creedal statement of Christianity has been, "Jesus Christ is Lord!" It is good, proper, and necessary that we make such a declaration.

Does the story of our life give the same testimony?

Imagine that the story of our life could be displayed on three large tables. On table one is the story of how we used our abilities. On table two is the story of how we responded to the various opportunities that crossed our path. On table three is a full financial disclosure, telling the story of our stewardship.

Will the story of the tables speak so loud as to drown out our declaration, "Jesus Christ is Lord!"?

Or will the story of the tables simply, humbly, add volume to our testimony, "Jesus Christ is Lord!"?

Treasures will tell the truthful tale.

Questions for reflection:

1) How does our culture view money and accumulation?

2) How has this cultural view impacted the "seeing" of those within the Church?

3) How does the story of your own "seeing" say about you?

4) What will the story of the tables say about you?

31. WORRY

"**Therefore** (in view of what Jesus said about treasure) **I tell you, do not worry about your life, what you will eat or drink, or about your body, what you will wear. Is not life more important than food, and the body more important than clothes? Look at the birds of the air; they do not sow or reap or store away in barns, yet your heavenly Father feeds them. Are you not of much more value than they? Who of you by worrying can add a single hour to his life? And why do you worry about clothes? See how the lilies of the field grow. They do not labor or spin. Yet I tell you that not even Solomon in all his splendor was dressed like one of these. If that is how God clothes the grass of the field, which is here today and tomorrow is thrown into the fire, will he not much more clothe you - you of little faith? So do not worry, saying, 'What shall we eat?' or 'What shall we drink?' or 'What shall we wear?' For the pagans run after all these things, and your heavenly Father knows that you need them. But seek first his kingdom and his righteousness and all these things will be given to you as well. Therefore do not worry about tomorrow, for tomorrow will worry about itself. Each day has enough trouble of its own.**"
(vss. 25-34)

After a convicting admonition about treasure, and the importance of how we see things of this life, Jesus now calls upon us to see so that we do not worry. He calls us to see the birds of the air and the flowers of the field. Not merely use the mechanism of sight so that we identify and describe the bird or the flower, but see the hidden, yet necessary, relationship of the Creator God to His creatures. This seeing reveals to us the sufficient care of the Heavenly Father for those who are His. We see the work of God in supplying the basic necessities of life. And in seeing, we know life. Not just life of the physical body, but life by every word that proceeds from the mouth of God. In seeing we know the special and unique value of the body: it is designed as the dwelling place of God; it is designed to be treated with respect and appropriate modesty as reflective of the glory and mystery of the Godhead. As such, it is unthinkable that the Creator Father would simply sit upon His throne as King of all things and watch such a miraculous design be degraded for lack of adequate clothing. Jesus encourages us to see and to know.

On the other side of this issue, like a single coin with two sides, are obligations placed upon us by the Scriptures. We are told that if a man will not work he should not expect to eat (**2 Thessalonians 3:10**); if a man does not provide for his immediate family he is worse than an unbeliever (**1 Timothy 5:8**); and a wise man plans an inheritance for his children (**Proverbs 13:22**).

The devil perverts these good and necessary things by appealing to our selfishness, suggesting uncertainty and fear.

He blinds us with the false glamour of earthly treasures. If our real enemy can get us to see only what we can touch, look at, and own, then he has created the potential for worry.

Through the process of worry this real enemy drives us to an even more intense expression of self-centeredness, deeper fear, and an obsession with the things of this earth. Soon we are living in a cycle of worry, with the intensity always trending upward. Before long we live in the constant frazzle of anxiety, projecting worry on everything, interpreting each event and each possibility through the filter of worry. In our worry we justify our frantic efforts at storing up earthly treasures. *"What IF?"* becomes the driving motto of our daily existence. *"What IF?"* becomes the lens through which we see into the future. *"What IF?"* move us to live outside of true reality.

With time this vicious cycle of worry becomes its own kind of infectious madness.

You have met such people...or maybe you are such a person. Someone shares some manner of good news and – "Well, you just wait. Even new cars break down." "Well, I used to know someone just like you: good news, good news, good news. And look what happened to them. They got cancer and died." "Sure, your kids will smile to your face, but God only knows what kinds of things they get in to when you're not around." "A raise? I'm sure the government is happy that they can now take even more money from you."

280

When someone's mind gets trapped in the vice of worry, the enemy of us all rejoices. He has succeeded, with our help, to kill, steal and destroy.

And the heavenly Father weeps.

Jesus begs us to hear him. He has already urged us to see life as it is meant to be seen and to treasure that which is most important. Only then will we discover we have no reason to worry.

No reason at all.

He gives us His word and points us to his works as supporting evidence. Listen: **"Ask the animals, they will teach you, or the birds of the air, and they will tell you…" (Job 12:7)**. **"The eyes of all look to you and you give them their food at the proper time. You open your hand and satisfy the desire of every living thing." (Psalm 145:15-16**). Jesus instructs us to look to the birds and look to the fields. The Creator God has put in place, by divine mandate, an ecology of life that insures adequate care is given to the birds and the beasts. This plan gives witness to His power, divine nature and providential care. How could we look at this great scheme of the Creator God, our Father, and disbelieve His ability and His desire to care for us?

How can we observe all this greatness, a greatness that has baffled and intrigued scientific pursuit for thousands of years, a greatness for that which perishes with the dying and disappears with the burning, and not believe? All of this greatness over that which does not bear His image. All of this greatness for that which is not His child. All this greatness on display so that we might learn to trust.

Since the Father shows such care over that which is today and tomorrow is not, how much more will He display His greatness as the Father for those who are adopted as His own through the blood of His Beloved Son?

The body He has given us is of unique design with an exclusive purpose. When God designed the human body, He did so as the Architect of His future home. A home in which He would incarnate Himself as God among men in the person of Jesus. A home in which He would tabernacle through the Holy Spirit. He will not allow that body, His home, to exist in the shame of neglect and nakedness (maybe we should remember that when we are choosing our clothing). Our reputation is not at stake; the glory of His Great Name is at stake. And He will not allow His Great Name to be degraded.

In **1 Timothy 5:8** we are given the seriousness responsibility of caring for our own family. Do we believe God would do any less? Did He not say that if we know how to respond appropriately to the needs and requests of our children, we can believe that He, too, knows even more how to take care of His own (**Luke 11:11-13**)?

Those without a heavenly Father – the pagans – are under the cruel deception that they must fend for themselves. Such a life has rightly been called the rat race. If life is all about self-care, then we must live a life of frenetic activity, aggressive accumulation, violent acquiring. No one can be allowed to get in the way. We must scratch and claw our way to the food trough if we are to survive at all.

Those who have a heavenly Father through the work of Christ have a Father who **"already knows."**

We must use caution lest we misread such a statement. This knowing does not create some kind of cosmic welfare state. We are obligated to be good stewards of the gifts and opportunities provided us by the Father. We are to work and live a productive life. We are not driven by worry or selfishness, but rather by trust and gratitude. Trust that the heavenly Father has provided the gifts and opportunities; gratitude that through this process we are insured basic provision.

Far too often we act as though God must provide and prepare the soil, plant the seeds, tend the garden, take up the harvest, process the harvest into a meal, and then serve us. And after that He should do the dishes!

We latch on with great zeal to any verse, no matter how badly taken out of context, that promises the painless and effortless provision of the Father to us.

A few years ago the Prayer of Jabez (**1 Chronicles 4:10**) generated such a frenzy. For a number of years I have heard **Philippians 4:19, "My God will meet all your needs according to his glorious riches in Christ Jesus"** quoted as some kind of magical potion. In more recent times it has been **Jeremiah 29:11** with its promise of prosperity. We pray, we quote, we sing these verses and others like them with very little effect.

God will not be manipulated into becoming an indulgent Father, not even by the misuse of His own Word.

To help clarify that truth, Jesus declares, **"Seek first the Kingdom of God and His righteousness."** We are invited to expend our energies to seek the Kingdom of God and His righteousness as the priority of life, not just as item #1 on some life list. We are to *seek Him*. We are not to seek after the provisions; we are to seek the Provider. We are not to seek earthly necessities; we are to seek Him as the only necessity. We are to seek first that which is His rather than seeking that which we want to claim as our own. We are to seek Him, not for the side benefits that become possible, but for the sake of knowing Him alone. We are to seek Him as though He is all that matters. When we do this, we are promised **"all these things."**

The kingdom of the world is fractured, competitive, and elusive. This kingdom is populated by those who are blinded and deluded, living in unnecessary confusion, pain and slavery. This kingdom demands payment. The slaves of this kingdom is taxed beyond ability, driven beyond strength, and discarded when no longer useful.

The Kingdom of Righteousness is ruled by a Father and populated by His children. In this Kingdom the Father has already paid the price for all that is most needed and most important. This Kingdom has an economy fully supplied and controlled by the Father, through which He provides abilities and opportunities for us to participate in the fulfillment of His purposes and plans. The Father makes all things possible and then absurdly declares to us, "Well done!" This is a Kingdom were life does not exist by the eating of bread alone. This is a Kingdom where the Father is filled with pleasure in creatively, surprisingly providing for His children.

In this Kingdom the Father-King rejoices in fulfilling the expressed purpose of His Son: **"I have come that they might have life, and have it to the full." (John 10:10)**

Questions for reflection:

1) How does our culture feed the monster of worry?

2) How has the church been influenced by this obsession with worry?

3) How has our misuse of Scripture only increased our obsession with worry?

4) Respond to this statement: "Worry is trading the 'I AM!' for 'What IF?'"

32. JUDGING

Matthew 7

"Don't judge me!"

We have all heard it. Most of us have said it. It is the reactionary declaration of a person who feels their actions are being unfairly criticized.

A number of years ago a young lady was involved in making some very poor decisions. Those decisions had the potential to bring very real and unnecessary pain to her life and the lives of many others. I challenged her to apply four principles to her decisions: seek the Lord in prayer; listen for the voice of the Lord in Scripture; accept the counsel of a mature Christian (*not* your best friend peer!); and seek the affirmation of the church.

Her response? "Don't you judge me!"

This next teaching of Jesus is probably the most quoted portion of the Bible and at the same time the most frequently misunderstood and misapplied portion of the Bible. There is a deep and convicting truth in this teaching. This teaching is not given to us to provide us with a great defensive reaction, but rather a sense of deep humility.

"Do not judge, or you too will be judged. For in the same way you judge others, you will be judged, and with the measure you use, it will be measured to you. Why do you look at the speck of sawdust in your brother's eye and pay no attention to the plank in your own eye? How can you say to your brother, 'Let me take the speck out of your eye,' when all the time there is a plank in your own eye? You hypocrite, first take the plank out of your own eye, and then you will see clearly to remove the speck from your brother's eye. Do not give dogs what is sacred; do not throw pearls to the pigs. If you do, they may trample them under their feet, and then turn and tear you to pieces." (7:1-6)

The first century audience heard this teaching with ears tuned by Old Testament understandings of judgment. The ancients saw the activity of the One True God like a coin: one side of the coin was the gracious and merciful offer of salvation; the other side of the coin was the authoritative application of punishment upon all who rejected the offer of salvation.

This was how the prophets were heard, including John the Baptist. Their messages were ones of "repent and receive God's merciful salvation; reject and be judged." Though the wording of their messages may not have been so explicit, the message was clear: repent and be saved, reject and be judged.

Ancient Jews understood this coin was God's alone. No one but God could save. Anyone who laid claim to the ability to forgive sins was immediately branded a blasphemous person (see **Mark 2:1-7**). The pronouncement of judgment was also seen as God's alone to make, even if that judgment required the use of human agency.

Even though this coin was seen as God's alone, ancient Jews understood it to be their responsibility to declare the truth of this coin – repent and receive the merciful salvation of the One True God; reject this merciful offer and receive the authoritative judgment of the One True God.

The audience heard this teaching in this context. Jesus gave this teaching from the same background.

What does this mean for us? How are we to hear and receive this teaching?

This teaching does not mean we abandon sound discernment. In just a few verses Jesus is going to urge us to exercise discernment – to make a judgment call - so we can recognize false prophets. This discernment is not for the sake of condemning the prophet; it is for the purpose of avoiding deception. The Bible presents numerous principles that speak to the issue of discernment. Discernment is never meant to equip us to exercise punishing judgment; it is given to us for the sake of maturing in wisdom and grace as we walk with Christ.

This teaching does not mean we abandon the exposure of sin. The Apostle Paul urged Timothy, **"Those who sin are to be rebuked publicly, so that the others may take warning." (1 Timothy 5:20).** In other portions of Scripture clear delineations are made between righteousness and sinfulness. Some behaviors, actions, attitudes and words are declared as righteous and some declared as sinful. We must not shy away from doing the same, declaring the truth in love **(Ephesians 4:15).**

This teaching does not mean we abandon the application of church discipline. According to the teaching of Jesus in **Matthew 18:15-20,** accountability between believers must begin as a personal endeavor. If this attempt at reconciliation is rejected, then one or two witnesses are to be added to the attempt. If this attempt at reconciliation is rejected, then the issue is to be brought before the church. If that attempt is rejected, then the offending person is to be viewed as an unbeliever and every effort is to be made to bring them to repentance and God's offer of merciful salvation. This entire process requires discernment and the exposure of sin. The purpose of this process is never punishing judgment: that is God's alone to exercise. The purpose of this process is the redemptive reconciliation of a fellow believer.

We are never in violation of this teaching of Jesus when we exercise Scriptural discernment to avoid deception, or when we declare sin to be sin, or when we exercise wise and appropriate church discipline.

We are in violation of this teaching of Jesus if we act as though the coin of salvation and judgment is ours to manipulate.

Only God saves. He alone has the authority to pronounce sins forgiven and all transgression erased. He alone has the power and authority to give new birth and to create a new person.

Only God has the authority to enact the judgment of punishment upon those who reject His merciful offer of salvation.

We must not act as though any of these actions is ours to do.

We are deceived if we believing it is okay to pronounce punishment upon those who offend us, those who show the slightest fault. Those who have a speck in their eye. We punish them by refusing to fellowship with them. We punish them by refusing to shake their hand. We punish them by gossiping about them through careless prayer requests. We make sure that in some way they know and feel our displeasure and disapproval. We block any opportunity they might have to serve (but are quick to accept their money).

By our actions we have placed a major offense in our own lives; we have become the people of the plank. Our action to take the authority to punish is in itself a far greater offense than their offense. In the words of Jesus, we, not them, have become hypocrites.

Jesus puts the burden of correction, not on the speck people but on us, the people of the plank. Get rid of the plank, get rid of the hypocrisy, stop the punishing judgment. Do these things and suddenly we will be reminded that the speck person is our brother or sister in Christ.

When we see the other person clearly, when we see them as a brother or sister in Christ, judgment vanishes. We are no longer interested in finding ways to punish them for their faults or even for their sins.

Instead, we see them as part of the family and respond: **"Brothers, if someone is caught in a sin, you who are spiritual should restore him gently. But watch yourself, or you also may be tempted." (Galatians 6:1**).

We must not be naïve. Not everyone will respond favorably to our living by the coin of God's economy. Some will respond unkindly, aggressively, and painfully. Some will accuse us of going soft on sin. Some will accuse us of ungodly compromise. Some will grow angry that we are not protecting their ideas and values. Some will rend us with their words, stomp on us with their attitude, and dismiss us from their fellowship. All in violation of this teaching of Christ.

Jesus tells us to withdraw from such people. We must not repeatedly expose that which is sacred to those who by their actions and reactions tarnish that which is holy. We must never reach for the coin, believing we have the right to punish them. We are to allow God to be God. He alone can save by His merciful grace. He alone has the authority to punish them in judgment.

At times we must simply leave some people under the hand of God.

Questions for reflection:

1) How is judgment being exercised in our culture?

2) How has the church mishandled this teaching of Jesus?

3) In your life and relationships, how have you usurped God's authority and applied punishing judgment to others?

4) What is a plank in your life? What must be done about it?

33. ASK, SEEK, KNOCK

Having worked in children's camps for nearly twenty years, raised two children, and now enjoying grandchildren, I have come to the following conclusion: Jesus must have just finished an encounter with a bunch of children then offered these words:

> **"Ask and it will be given to you; seek and you will find; knock and the door will be opened to you. For everyone who asks receives; he who seeks finds; and to him who knocks the door will be opened. Which of you, if his son asks for bread, will give him a stone? Or if he asks for a fish, will give him a snake? If you, then, though you are evil, know how to give good gifts to your children, how much more will your Father in heaven give good gifts to those who ask him! So in everything do to others what you would have them do to you, for this sums up the Law and the Prophets."** (7-12)

Ask and keep on asking. Seek and keep on seeking. Knock and keep on knocking (certainly sounds like the relentlessness of a four-year old!). Keep at it: then success! It is given, found, and opened.

I must confess this portion of the Sermon on the Mount troubles me. On the one hand I have made simple, one-time requests and had those requests dramatically answered within days. On the other hand, I have made some requests desperately, repeatedly and...*nothing.*

On the one hand the Father knew my need before I asked and was pleased to simply supply. On the other hand, my Father seemed to be difficult to persuade and resistant to respond.

I am confident I am not alone in having such a prayer story to tell.

I am prayerful this lesson enlarges our understanding of the concept of prayer and puts to rest the troubles I have described.

Jesus presents us with a simple truth in the larger context of prayer: *prayer involves varying urgencies and varying needs.*

When Jesus told us to ask and keep asking he is giving us the simplest expression of prayer. Like a son asking a father for food: a simple request that only requires a simple transaction.

Each day we are faced with such simplicities. Jesus described these simplicities just moments ago: food, drink, and clothing (6:25-34). He addressed these simplicities in the model prayer: **"Give us today our daily bread"** (6:11). Simple asking and simple, adequate provision. A daily interaction of dependence for those things necessary for that day.

We must remember that the only frame of reference for the first audience is the Old Testament. In the Old Testament this simple ask/supply is seen in a dramatic way. After the powerful exodus the children of Israel wandered in the wilderness for decades. God, as Father, knew their need. He provided food every day, provided water in miraculous ways, and preserved their shoes and clothing.

We can trust this truth today. He knows we need food, shelter, and clothing. We will not live as orphans or experience complete destitution. Our Father knows and will provide. He will never let the family name be disgraced.

Jesus also tells us to seek and to keep on seeking, expressing a different level of urgency with a different targeted need. Jesus never taught us to seek after food, drink or clothing. He said pagans seek after such things, implying they put too much urgency and importance on such things. Isn't it true that most of us seek these simple things? That we place too high a value on these things? We seek these things but then merely ask for the greater things of God. No wonder we live in spiritual poverty and confusion.

Many well intended Christians spend time seeking after some kind of sign: some of the stories border on the absurd. Jesus, on two occasions, responded this way when asked for a sign; **"A wicked and adulterous generation asks for a miraculous sign!" (Matthew 12:36; 16:4)**. On both occasions he then pointed back to the record of Scripture as enough.

I have encountered Christians who actively sought after spiritual gifts. The Bible does not encourage such seeking but simply states: **"All these** (spiritual gifts) **are the work of one and the same Spirit, and he gives them to each one just as he determines."** (1 Corinthians 12:11)

I have watched as Christians have sought, in desperate ways and often for prolonged periods, the infilling of the Holy Spirit. Once again, seeking where only asking would suffice: **"If you then, though you are evil, know how to give good gifts to your children, how much more will your Father in heaven give the Holy Spirit to those who ask?" (Luke 11:13)** Jesus told the disciples just before his ascension: **"…wait for the gift my Father promised, which you have heard me speak about,"**, referring to the gift of the Holy Spirit.

Jesus did tell us to seek the Kingdom of God and God's righteousness (6:33). The Kingdom of God is of greater urgency than life's basic simplicities. The Kingdom is of greater need and of greater value than food, drink and clothing. This Kingdom we seek is like a treasure in a field or a priceless pearl (**Matthew 13:44-45**). This Kingdom is worthy of our most dramatic decision, and worthy of each effort put forth in seeking. This Kingdom is worth tenacious involvement, an ever-broadening search pattern, and a relentlessness that will not give up until the sought item is found.

Jesus taught us to pray, **"Your Kingdom come"** and encouraged us to seek that Kingdom. The Apostle Paul stated, **"The kingdom of God is not a matter of eating and drinking, but of righteousness, peace and joy in the Holy Spirit..." (Romans 14:17).**

Consider: **"Without faith it is impossible to please God, because anyone who comes to him must believe that he exists and that he rewards those who earnestly seek him." (Hebrews 11:6).**

Again, the Apostle Paul: **"My purpose is that they may be encouraged in heart and united in love, so that they may have the full riches of complete understanding, in order that they may know the mystery of God, namely, Christ, *in whom are hidden all the treasures of wisdom and knowledge." (Colossians 2:2-3** *emphasis added*).

These great treasures of the Kingdom and righteousness are not simply given. These great treasures are found as we seek them out. As we give ourselves to the reading of Scripture suddenly the Holy Spirit will highlight a portion. In that portion will be found a great treasure, a priceless pearl, the treasure of Christ. Had we sat in a chair and asked for this treasure without seeking, we would have lived in disappointment and confusion. Only when we seek these treasures are we promised a great moment of discovery.

Jesus takes us to yet another level: knock and keep on knocking. Knocking is a straightforward process with an equally straightforward purpose.

Among the ancient Jews, knocking on the doorway is the beginning of hospitality. The door would be opened and the guest invited in. Feet would be washed, food and drink served, a special garment presented, and safety would be assured. The host made sure of it all.

Knocking in prayer?

Could it be that Jesus is encouraging us to understand that when we desire entrance into the presence of the Father all we need do is *knock*? We are not coming to ask: that is another thing entirely. We are not on a great search: that, too, is another thing. All we desire is to be in the presence of the Father. To be refreshed by His presence. To be embraced by His Holiness. To live in the peace and security of His Sovereignty. Him. Just Him. Nothing else, nothing less, and nothing more. Not stuff. No relentless pursuit. Him. Just him. Jesus promised that when we knock the door will be opened.

Knocking puts us in the presence of the Father. The Father, as host, gives us gifts for which we did not ask and opens treasures which we did not seek. We experience a moment of extravagant grace.

Through *asking*, God comes to our lives with His providential care. This act is not a divine indulgence. This response is a divine gift.

Through *seeking*, God rewards us with treasures of great grandeur. Invaluable treasures. Treasures worthy of our most diligent and sacrificial search. Treasures worthy of the exchange of our very life.

Through *knocking*, God grants access into His very presence. There we experience the hospitality of His extravagant grace. What words could describe such an awesome encounter?

Jesus makes another left turn without use of a signal: **"...do to others as you would have them do to you..."** What? Wait a minute! Aren't we talking about prayer?

Slowly the lights come on. "Oh, I get it. The life of prayer is of little value – nothing given, nothing found, no door opened – if we live crassly, carelessly, selfishly among our neighbors. If we hold them to a different relational standard than the standard to which we hold ourselves. If we treat others in contrast with how we expect God to treat us in response to our asking, seeking, and knocking."

This teaching of Jesus on prayer helps our prayers become meaningful and effective. This teaching of Jesus on prayer helps us see the connection between our prayers and our treatment of others.

Through this teaching on prayer we are invited into a fuller experience of the Kingdom of God.

Questions for reflection:

1) How does our culture treat the idea of prayer? How does that idea line up with this teaching of Jesus on prayer?

2) How has the church given evidence of confusion in the urgency and values of asking, seeking, and knocking?

3) Think a moment about your own prayer practice. In what ways have you been confused regarding asking, seeking, and knocking?

4) What steps need to be taken to align your prayer practice with this teaching of Jesus?

34. GATES

I have a fence around my back yard. It has four gates: two walk-through gates located at each end of the house, and two double gates in the back. These gates are meant to give controlled access to my back yard. They are installed in the fence to keep out or keep in while providing entrance and exit.

The audience gathered around Jesus were familiar with such utilitarian uses of a gate. They also had a broader understanding of gates. They, and the generations before them, understood the use and value of the city gate. It was a central part of community life. The elders of the city often sat at the gate where they engaged in debate, settled disputes, and negotiated contracts. Crowds gathered around the gate to watch and to listen. Above the gate was a place for a watchman to stand guard. Within the passages on either side of the gate where chambers for those guards to rest during their down time. The gate was often the place where punishment was given to those who transgressed the law. The city gate was closed at night to provide security for those within the city.

When Jesus states, **"Enter through the narrow gate. For wide is the gate and broad is the road that leads to destruction, and many enter through it. But small is the gate and narrow the road that leads to life, and only a few**

find it," (vss. 13-14) this first audience immediately formed thought pictures of a city gate. Jesus knew this about his audience: he knew how they heard him. A true understanding of Jesus' teaching requires that we, too, embrace this ancient understanding of a gate.

Jesus presents a divisive truth with only two choices for how life can be lived. Each way has a gate, an entry point, and each gate leads to contrasting places. The contrast is so great that any blending of the two gates is impossible. Two gates, two paths going toward different destinations, with no way to live a little from the narrow way and a little from the broad path.

Fallen human nature does not receive this truth. We desire to create a custom path. A path that pleases us and expresses how we want to live and what we choose to value. We want authority over the entry of this path: we decide how easy or hard the entry will be. We want to dictate the destination of our path: our path may wander far and wide but will somehow end with us going to a better place. We want to set the terms and conditions of the journey along our custom path. When Jesus says there are only two gates, only two paths and only two contrasting destinations we immediately reject the idea and counter with our own version. We want a journey with which we can be pleased and a destination with which God is pleased. We want to go our way and yet end up in His Place.

What folly.

Recently I made a trip from my home in Virginia to downtown Indianapolis, a trip of over 600 miles. The desired destination set the path I must take. I could not select I-95 south out of Virginia and hope to arrive in Indianapolis, no matter how much I preferred the scenery of the Carolinas. I could not pick a little of this route and a little of that route to patch together a custom route to Indianapolis. I could not say, "I think I will take a little of the Interstate that goes to the Grand Canyon, and little of the Highway that goes into the redwood forest, and a stretch of road that leads to the Aquarium in Corpus Christi. Yea, that would make a great path to Indianapolis!"

Yet we attempt to do such a thing with the journey of life.

When Jesus speaks of a wide gate, the people thought of a gate which allowed entry for anything. Come and go as you please. Could it be that Jesus meant to give a word picture of a self-centered, careless way of life? No engaging debates, no settling of disputes, no negotiated contracts, no punishment of law breakers. Above this gate are several signs: "whatever makes you happy," "have it your way," "happiness is the highest goal," "do as you please," "If you don't care neither do we." This gate required no thoughtfulness. This gate only requires movement. This gate is so wide that it allows each person in the crowd to believe they are making a unique expression of their individuality just like everybody else.

Once through this wide gate the way is described as a broad path. So broad, in fact, that Jesus used a word to describe this path that was often used to describe a field.

Think about it. No defined limits. No landmarks by which to determine location or progress. Only the opportunity for confusion and lostness disguised as freedom. No restriction of movement and no provision for safety.

The wide gate provides entry into a meaningless and purposeless life. The broad path is the perfect place for those who would "eat, drink, and be merry for tomorrow we die." This broad path is the perfect place for those willing to live in the delusions of a self-centered life.

The broad path is the perfect place for destruction to lurk over the horizon.

Jesus uses a word for destruction with a rather restricted meaning. This word is not used to describe a moment of pain, loss, or discomfort, but rather to describe eternal damnation.

This word describes the inevitable, irreversible destination for those who choose the wide gate and broad path. Every path goes somewhere and this broad path goes to destruction. You cannot enter at this gate, walk this path, and arrive somewhere else. This wide gate, broad path, and final destruction are the unholy trinity of a life lived for self.

Thank God there is another way.

Jesus describes this way as having a narrow gate leading to a narrow way.

The narrow gate offers a point of focus, a place of controlled access, and a place where all the important functions of a gate might occur.

No one just wanders in at this gate, uncertain of where they are of where they intend to go. This gate must be found, and once found, a clear purpose is expressed by entering through it. The judicial and communal activities around this gate help influence such a decision. At this gate sins are exposed, transgressions are judged, and forgiveness is expressed. The old life is cast aside and a new life is embraced. A new covenant is enacted. Entrance at this gate is not a secretive thing: entering is publicly done and publicly known. Those who entered before you *know.* Those who welcome you *know.* And you *know.* And you are *known.*

Once conditions for entry are met, and entry is made, life enters into a defined space. Anyone may choose to enter, but not anything goes. This narrow life has boundaries. There are discernable landmarks and clearly marked limits, by which we are assured of our position on the path and by which we might have a sense of progress.

While it is impossible to understand everything at once, there is no need for confusion. Questions do not lead to uncertainty, for the answers are framed in the narrowness of the journey. This narrowness is not experienced as a restriction or a short leash. This narrowness actually creates a sense of true and recognized freedom. "I was *there*; I am now *here*; and I am going to *that*."

The mode of entry and the narrowness of the journey create a perfect environment for those who desire a meaningful and purposeful life.

The mode of entry and the narrowness of this journey create a perfect way for any who so choose to invest their life in making a difference in this world.

The mode of entry and the narrowness of this journey create a perfect place for those who desire to live an extraordinary life, a life beyond themselves.

The mode of entry and the narrowness of this journey create an adventure of experiencing a life filled with the Holy Spirit.

This narrow way is a place of unshakable security and a place of the promises fulfilled. This narrow way leads to a destination while allowing the destination to begin *now*.

This narrow way is a place of life leading to life.

Over the horizon is nothing but life - glorious, expanding, awesome life.

N.T. Wright paints a picture of this life: "Made for spirituality, we wallow in introspection. Made for joy, we settle for pleasure. Made for justice, we clamor for vengeance. Made for relationship, we insist on our own way.

Made for beauty, we are satisfied with sentiment. But new creation has already begun. The sun has begun to rise. Christians are called to leave behind, in the tomb of Jesus Christ, all that belongs to the brokenness and incompleteness of the present world. It is time, in the power of the Spirit, to take up our proper role, our fully human role, as agents, heralds, and stewards of the new day that is dawning. That, quite simply, is what it means to be Christian: to follow Jesus Christ into the new world, God's new world, which he has thrown open to us." [28]

Jesus is the Way: enter through Him, follow Him and find life both now and forever.

---

[28] N. T. Wright, *Simply Christian: Why Christianity Makes Sense,* (NY, NY: Harper One, 2006), pg. 237.

Questions for reflection:

1) How does our culture respond to the idea of 'two paths, two destinations'?

2) What influence has this culture had upon the message of the Church on this issue?

3) How would you define the journey of your life before Christ?

4) How would you describe your journey with Christ?

5) When was the last time you shared your story with someone else?

35. FRUIT

"Watch out for false prophets. They come to you in sheep's clothing, but inwardly are ferocious wolves. By their fruit you will know them. Do people gather grapes from thorn bushes, or figs from thistles? Likewise every good tree bears good fruit, but a bad tree bears bad fruit. Every tree that does not bear good fruit is cut down and thrown into the fire. Thus, by their fruit you will recognize them. Not everyone who says to me, 'Lord, Lord,' will enter the kingdom of heaven, but only he who does the will of my Father who is in heaven. Many will say to me on that day, 'Lord, Lord, did we not prophesy in your name, and in your name drive out demons and perform many miracles?' Then I will tell them plainly, 'I never knew you. Away from me, you evildoers!'" (vss. 15-23)

The audience of Jesus had a basic understanding of the work of a prophet: to speak the word of the Lord which included pronouncements of blessing, warning, woe and calls to repentance. At times the work of the prophet involved the foretelling of future events in connection to these blessings or warnings.

The prophet had the mandate of God as his only and sufficient authority. No government or civic organization granted a prophet's license. The true prophet answered only to God who gave him the prophetic mandate. The mark of a true prophet was not the claim to be a prophet nor the words spoken. The marks of a true prophet were that prophet's obedience to the Laws of God and the fulfillment of his prophetic words.

> "If a prophet, or one who foretells by dreams, appears among you and announces to you a miraculous sign or wonder, and if the sign or wonder of which he has spoken takes place, and he says, 'Let us follow other gods' (gods you have not known) 'and let us worship them,' you must not listen to the words of that prophet or dreamer. It is the LORD your God you must follow, and him you must revere. Keep his commands and obey him; serve him and hold fast to him. That prophet or dreamer must be put to death, because he preached rebellion against the LORD your God."
> (Deuteronomy 13:1-2,4-5)

> "A prophet who presumes to speak in my name anything I have not commanded him to say, or a prophet who speaks in the name of other gods, must be put to death. You may say to yourselves, 'How can we know when a message has not been spoken by the LORD?' If what a prophet proclaims in the name of the LORD does not take place or come true, that is a message the LORD has not

spoken. That prophet has spoken presumptuously.
Do not be afraid of him." (Deuteronomy 18:20-22)

Even with this divinely ordered zero tolerance for false
prophets, such prophets still arose. The power and prestige
of being a prophet appealed to the lust for power and the
desire for fame. The prophets manipulated the people with
cruelty or comforted the people with false hopes. Theirs
words found a ready audience: an audience wanting to hear
such messages.

Such an audience can still be found:

> "The time will come when men will not put up with
> sound doctrine. Instead, to suit their own desires,
> they will gather around them a great number of
> teachers to say what their itching ears want to hear.
> They will turn their ears away from truth and turn
> aside to myths." (2 Timothy 4:3-4)

I have been involved in the world of the church for nearly 50
years. During that time, I have seen the itching ears and false
prophet come together on more than one occasion. Very
seldom have those with itching ears said, "I want to live a
wicked life and need someone to tell me that is ok." Very
seldom has a 'prophet' stood before any group of people and
stated, "Yield to your most base desires. God will not care!"
What I have heard and seen is far more subtle and alluring.
Those with itching ears wanted their self-righteousness

affirmed. And some preacher will get up and provide such affirmation.

Years ago I listened as a church leader preached. He was presenting a good, solid message but had little response or support from his audience (mostly pastors). He began to rant on the issues dear to that denomination: issues that were nonexistent in the lives of the people who were in that audience. Now he had vocal support! Now the itching ears were being scratched. Now the marks of self-righteousness were being highlighted.

More than once I have observed such an exchange. It was disturbing to me then and is disturbing to me yet today.

Jesus says we should watch out for false prophets. False prophets never wear an ID badge: "FALSE PROPHET". They are never quite that obvious. They come in disguise and only those who exercise discernment will recognize them. These false prophets are often self-appointed, driven by self-interest, and operate from a selfish agenda. Their words may sound true and they even quote proof texts from the Bible. Their words have a ring of familiarity about them. But *watch out.* Under the thin veneer of deception is the true nature of the beast. Remember: those who are false are shallow: that which seems right and good is only skin deep. So be patient and pay attention.

"Test everything." (1 Thessalonians 5:21)

"Dear friends, do not believe every spirit, but test the spirits to see whether they are from God, because many false prophets have gone out into the world. This is how you can recognize the Spirit of God: Every spirit that acknowledges that Jesus Christ has come in the flesh is from God...." (1 John 4:1-2)

Translated into our cultural context this message might sound like this:

"When the new wonder-kid skyrockets to fame in the world of the church, when his words are smooth and persuasive, when it is reported that he is suddenly a best-selling author, when the TV camera reveals a massive audience – be patient and pay attention. Time will reveal the truth to those who are discerning. If the revealed truth shows him to be God-called, God-appointed, God-anointed then Praise the Lord! If the revealed truth exposes him to be filled with self-interest, then beware: all the good is only skin deep and the true beastly nature will soon be known.

Don't join the fan club too quickly. Don't buy the books too quickly. Don't subscribe to the newsletter too quickly. Don't send money too quickly. Watch and wait."

Jesus then illustrates this truth with the story of the trees. Please, *please,* don't think for a moment Jesus is giving us a hard-and-fast botany lesson. One man approached me about this passage some years ago. He took some exception to these verses because he had personally experienced a good fruit tree that had produced a bad piece of fruit or vice versa. Jesus is not saying that in the world of botany a good fruit tree will never produce a bad piece of fruit or that a bad tree will never produce a good piece of fruit.

Jesus is giving us a principled example to enforce his warning: watch out for those who are false. He is telling us there is a way to know the true nature of the prophet.

Examine what is produced.

Deception may last for a time but the true nature will always be revealed. Remember, the sheep's skin is only skin deep. A moment will come when the true nature of the beast is exposed. A time will come when it is clear to all that this prophet only intended to devour.

There are many such prophets in the world. They look like a sheep but with time the smell of a wolf is apparent. They devour: take money for those of simple means and build themselves great mansions, exotic cars, yachts, private jets and exclusively tailored suits. Words of a sheep but the behavior of a wolf.

Watch out.

Jesus brings this lesson to a hard conclusion.

The doing of good works, even doing them in his name, is no guarantee of a righteous character.

There is a distinct difference between good deeds and righteous works.

What marks the difference is the motive.

> **"I may speak in different languages of people of even of angels, but if I do not have love, I am only a noisy bell or a crashing cymbal. I may have the gift of prophecy, I may understand all the secret things of God and have all knowledge, and I may have faith so great I can move mountains. But even with all these things, if I do not have love, then I am nothing. I may give away everything I have, and I may even give my body as an offering to be burned. But I gain nothing if I do not have love." (1 Corinthians 13:1-3 NCV)**

"Such an act is good whether done in love or not if it supplies a need: but without love it cannot be a righteous act; without his really wanting to do it, it is not a moral deed at all." [29]

Without the presence of divine love in the heart, our good deeds are driven by the same nature that drives the false prophet: *self-interest.*

Without the presence of divine love in the heart, we are all wearing the deception of a sheep skin.

---

[29] Arthur Custance, *Time and Eternity,* The Doorway Papers, vol. 6, (Grand Rapids, MI: Zondervan, 1977), pg. 171.

Only divine love can remove the disguise. Only divine love can change the inner nature. Only divine love can make us true.

Only divine love can cause our good deeds to become righteous works.

Only the transforming work of divine love in and through us can change the words of Jesus on that day from "I don't know you" to "Welcome home and well done!"

Let us hear and heed this teaching of Jesus.

Watch out for deceptions around us.

Watch out for deceptions within us.

Submit to the transforming power of divine love.

Questions for reflection:

1) Our culture is filled with deception for the sake of personal gain. What are some recent examples?

2) How has the Western church imitated this behavior? What impact has such imitation had upon the witness of the church?

3) How has your own life been challenged by self-interests at the cost of truth?

4) What actions need to be taken to improve discernment in this area?

5) Respond to this statement: "Without the presence of divine love in the heart, we are all wearing the deception of a sheep skin."

36. FOUNDATIONS

Knowing the nature of fallen humanity, Jesus concludes his teaching with strong words. These words give us no avenue of escape.

> **"Therefore everyone who hears these words of mine and puts them into practice is like a wise man who built his house on the rock. The rain came down, the streams rose, and the winds blew and beat against that house; yet it did not fall, because it had its foundation on the rock. But everyone who hears these words of mine and does not put them into practice is like a foolish man who built his house on sand. The rain came down, the streams rose, and the winds blew and beat against that house, and it fell with a great crash."** (vss. 24-27)

One builder is declared as wise. This builder listened to those with experience and knowledge. This builder submitted to a master builder as an apprentice. He understood that building a house was more than putting together materials to create a structure. This wise builder understood the house was a symbol of his life: it spoke of his hopes, dreams and his future. His decision to build a house declared his readiness to enter manhood.

Several years ago while in Israel I had an interesting conversation with a native of Israel. I learned that in the Middle Eastern culture a man must take a home before he can take a wife. Building a house declared readiness for marriage, family, grandchildren and the eventual seat as patriarch of one's own clan. Building a house expressed the value a man placed on a thoughtful, well-ordered life. It declared his readiness to enter adulthood with all its responsibilities and privileges.

Jesus uses this culturally understood example to make a strong point: those who listen to and practice his words are like that wise builder. They have listened and learned. They are willing to submit to apprenticeship. They are forward thinkers. They are intentional and purposeful about pursuing a desired future and understand that such a future begins right here, right now. These individuals do not see the teachings of Jesus as a moralistic check list to complete. They hear the teachings of Jesus describing a life to be lived.

The teachings of Jesus offer a life of stability and security in ways that matter most. This promised life is not without raging flood waters and howling wind. This life will endure the storm, the flood, and the wind. This life will endure the sudden, catastrophic chaos of circumstances. This life will *be* once the storm becomes a *has been*. This life might be soaked by the rain, mucked by the flood and rattled by the wind but still *is*.

The teachings of Jesus have this power in the life of those listen.

> **"Get rid of all moral filth and the evil that is so prevalent and humbly accept the word planted in you, which can save you. Do not merely listen to the word, and so deceive yourselves. Do what it says. Anyone who listens to the word but does not do what it says is like a man who looks at his face in a mirror and, after looking at himself, goes away and immediately forgets what he looks like. But the man who looks intently into the perfect law that gives freedom, and continues to do this, not forgetting what he has heard, but doing it – he will be blessed in what he does." (James 1:21-25)**

Then there is the other builder, whom Jesus declared to be a fool. This fool is the picture of a man who ignores the accumulated knowledge and experience of those who have gone before him. He refuses apprenticeship: he has no sense of need. He, too, wants an adult life with bride, family and future. He believes the lie that he is the exception and need not be bothered with the costs of good house building. He does not do the necessary work of seeking the right place to establish his life. He does not do the necessary work to create a good beginning for a successful future. He wants what he wants and wants it now.

He takes shortcuts. These shortcuts are hidden from view: from the street his house and the house of the wise builder appear similar. His house may actually appear more lavish and spectacular. This is only because he transferred expense and effort from the foundation to the appearance. After visiting both houses, a guest may walk away believing the houses are similar in function and construction.

One might look upon the house of the wise builder and accuse him of over-building his house. "So much unnecessary expense and effort. The other house is a better example of frugal, yet sufficient, house building." The fool's house becomes the new minimum standard for other hopeful men.

Such is the way of humanity.

If given the opportunity to choose a lesser way with the same promised results, we will jump at the chance and declare, "What a deal!" Especially when that lesser way is in such harmony with our selfish agenda and still allows us to look good.

Too many lives take this lesser way. It looks good, works for a while, and numbs the senses to the impending crisis.

And then the crisis happens. The inevitable storm sweeps in.

A child is in trouble with the law. The downsizing at work costs your job. Your best friend whispers suspicions about your spouse. Your favorite neighbor is diagnosed with cancer. Your parents have increasing needs that place stressful demands on life.

The list grows long.

The news comes like a few dramatic days of rain, a few traumatic moments of flooding, and a decisive gust of wind.

And your house, your whole world, collapses.

The collapse is a great crash.

The devastation is not just to the embarrassment of the builder. The devastation shatters trust among family and friends. Neighbors and associates are angered: they had patterned their house after his. Should they now expect the same collapse?

The builder is exposed as a fool. His future is gone: he will never take his seat as the patriarch of his own clan. The cost of those harmless shortcuts has now driven his entire life into bankruptcy.

Such is the description of someone who has heard the teachings of Jesus and ignored them. A day is coming, a moment is coming, when such a life will be devastated beyond recovery. There is no putting such a life back together except by the amazing grace of God.

Two men, one wise the other foolish.

One storm, common to both.

Two houses, one built well the other built poorly.

One storm, common to both.

Two contrasting results.

A great stand and a devastating crash.

How will our stories end? Wisely of foolishly? Will the storms of life cause our collapse or will we stand firm?

What we do with the teachings of Jesus predicts the answer.

Choose wisely.

EPILOGUE

Preaching this series of messages had a transformative effect upon my life. I am forever grateful for the grace of God that came to me through His Word.

Mine has been an interesting journey. I was called to preach in the third grade and called to Christ at the age of fourteen (I know – God did it in reverse order! I have left it to Him to straighten out). I began preaching in my Junior year of High School: that was almost forty years ago.

For a number of years I was guilty of preaching the accepted party line. I preached those things that were safe. I preached in a way that was considered proper. I was doing as I had seen, heard, and been taught to do.

Then something began to change.

Slowly at first, then with increasing swiftness.

I began to discover the depths of the Word on my own. Various authors challenged my thinking; many of those authors are listed in the bibliography.

This journey of discovery is increasingly intense, challenging, convicting, and exhilarating all at once. The Bible has never been more alive to me than now.

This book comes from my journey. While I make no claim to have exhausted the depths of the Sermon on the Mount, I testify that this Sermon has changed me in ways that nothing else has and in ways that will never be undone.

I invite you to enter such a journey. I hope this simple book encourages your journey of discovery.

HOLES

"I've noticed in my being

Some Holy Spirit holes

And searching where I'm draining

I wonder where He goes.

Why am I always needing

Another quart to fill

If I'm intent on living

In the center of God's will

Maybe as I'm sinning

He just starts to leak out

Or maybe I exhale Him

Each time I curse or shout

Or possible reversal

And opposite is true

That when I am a blessing

He flows from me to you.

Perhaps I'm like a vapor

And I humidify

A world that's gotten arid

And wilting from the dry

But either way please fill me

From springs there up above

For this is my desire

A taste I've come to love."

By Elliot Sexton Fuller, *Poetry in Devotion,* pg. 284

BIBLIOGRAPHY -

Abegg, Martin G. Jr. Cook, Edward M. Wise, Michael O. *The Dead Sea Scrolls: A New Translation.* Harper Collins Publishers, 1996, 2005.

Black, David Alan & Lea, Thomas D. *The New Testament: Its Background and Message.* Nashville, TN: Broadman & Holman Publishers, 2003.

Bonhoeffer, Dietrich; *Life Together Prayer Book of the Bible.* Minneapolis, MN: Fortress Press, 2005.

Boone, Dan; *A Charitable Discourse: talking about the things that divide us.* Kansas City, MO: Beacon Hill Press, 2010.

Chambers, Oswald. *Studies In The Sermon On The Mount.* Grand Rapids, MI: Discovery House Publishers, 1995.

Custance, Arthur;

>   *Man in Adam and in Christ,* The Doorway Papers, vol. three. Grand Rapids, MI: the Zondervan Corporation, 1975

>   *Time and Eternity,* the Doorway Papers, vol. six. Grand Rapids, MI: the Zondervan Corporation, 1977

Earle, Ralph and Laaser, Mark. *The Pornography Trap.* Kansas, MO: Beacon Hill Press, 2002.

Fuller, Elliot Sexton. *Poetry in Devotion: Be Still and Know That I Am God.* Printed in the United States by Bookmasters, 2017.

Hall, Laurie *An Affair of the Mind.* Colorado Springs, CO: Focus on the Family Publishers, 1996.

Harris, Ralph W., Executive Editor. *The Complete Biblical Library.* Springfield, MO: World Library Press, Inc., 1989.

Lucado, Max. *Come Thirsty.* Nashville, TN: Word Publishing Group, a division of Thomas Nelson Publishers, 2004.

Marston, Gaye Berkshire. *The Truth About Me.* c. Gaye Marston 2017.

McArthur, John. *the Power of Suffering.* Wheaton, IL: Victor Books, A Division of Scripture Press Publications Inc., 1995.

McManus, Erwin Raphael. *An Unstoppable Force: daring to become the church GOD had in mind.* Loveland, CO: Group Publishing Inc., 2001.

Nee, Watchman. *The Normal Christian Life.* Fort Washington, PA: CLC Publications, 2009 by CLC Ministries International with permission from Tyndale House Publishers, Inc.

Oden, Thomas C. *The Living God; Systematic Theology: vol One.* Peabody, MA: Prince Press, 1987.

Pell, Edward Leigh. *Our Troublesome Religious Questions.* New York, Chicago, Toronto, London, Edinburgh: Fleming Revell Company, 1916.

Ryle, J. C. *Holiness: Its Nature, Hindrances, Difficulties and Roots.* Cambridge: Cambridge University Press, 1959.

Sproul, R.C. *The Holiness of God: study guide.* Orlando, FL: Ligonier Ministries Curriculum Series, 1988.

Towns, Elmer. *Knowing God Through Fasting.* Shippensburg, PA: Destiny Image Publishers, Inc., 2002.

Vail, Eric M. *Atonement and Salvation: the Extravagance of God's Love.* Kansas City, MO: Beacon Hill Press, 2016.

White, James Emery. *Meet Generation Z; Understanding and Reaching the New Post-Christian World.* Grand Rapids, MI: Baker Books, a Division of Baker Publishing Group, 2017.

White, Reginald, E.O. *They Teach Us To Pray.* New York: Harper and Brothers Publishers, 1957.

Wigoder, Geoffrey, General Editor. *Illustrated Dictionary and Concordance of the Bible* Jerusalem Publishing House Ltd., 1986.

Wiseman, Neil B. *The Untamed God: Unleashing the Supernatural in the Body of Christ.* Kansas City, MO: Beacon Hill Press, 1997.

Wright, N. T.

> *The Lord and His Prayer.* Grand Rapids, MI: William
> B. Eerdmans Publishing Company, 1996.
>
> *Simply Jesus: A New Vison of Who He Was, What He
> Did, and Why He Matters.* NY, NY: Harper Collins
> Publishers, 2011.
>
> *Simply Christian: Why Christianity Makes Sense.* NY,
> NY: Harper One, an Imprint of Harper Collins
> Publishers, 2006.

Young, Ed. *Outrageous, Contagious Joy: Five Big Questions to
Help You Discover One Great Life.* NY, NY: The Berkley
Publishing Group; published by the Penguin Group, 2007.

Made in the USA
Middletown, DE
02 February 2023

22916903R00201